Sweet I

*Interviewer*
Alan Titchmarsh

*Researcher*
Kate Payne

*Production Team*
Sue Coombs
Sue Martin
Imran Vittachi
Simon Robinson

*Production Manager*
Kathryn West

*Commissioning Editor*
Helen Alexander

*Associate Producer*
Anuradha Vittachi

*Produced and Directed by*
Peter Armstrong

# Sweet Inspiration

### Introduced by Alan Titchmarsh

## Hodder & Stoughton
LONDON SYDNEY AUCKLAND

The extract from Christopher Fry, *Selected Plays* (May 1985) on
p. 110 is published by permission of Oxford University Press.

British Library Cataloguing in Publication Data

A CIP catalogue record for this title is available
from the British Library.

ISBN 0 340 62757 3

Typeset by Hewer Text Composition Services, Edinburgh
Printed and bound in Great Britain by Cox & Wyman Ltd.
Reading

Hodder and Stoughton Ltd,
A division of Hodder Headline PLC
338 Euston Road
London NW1 3BH

# CONTENTS

# INTRODUCTION

## by

## Alan Titchmarsh

The television chat show comes in for more criticism than almost any other type of programme except those that are generously furnished with sex and violence. It's not only the personality of the host that may lead to insults being hurled at the screen; one of the greatest frustrations is that the programme can turn into a sort of verbal sheep-dip. The conversations are too short. The interviewee barely seems to have got going before the presenter's voice or the editor's knife comes in to keep things moving along. There's still a feeling in some quarters that the attention span of the viewing public is little more than one and a half minutes. It's not always a bad premise in that it prevents dreary old bores from going on for half an hour and it also concentrates the mind of both the questioner and the victim. But it does mean that in-depth conversation is unlikely.

That is why I was so keen to tackle a programme like *Sweet Inspiration* which would allow public figures to talk about their deepest feelings during half an hour of conversation. In reality we often talked for much longer, but that meant we had an even greater choice when it came to keeping in the good bits.

*Sweet Inspiration* might just as easily be called *Desert Island Hymns*, for the interviewees were asked to choose five or six hymns which, during their lives, had come to have a special significance.

The conversation revolved around faith in the broadest sense of the word. I was curious to discover what had influenced my guests in their development as individuals on all kinds of levels, not just their religious beliefs.

I have always found that talking to a person who has a deep and unquestioning faith leaves me feeling faintly uneasy and rather inadequate. I think many viewers, too, find it hard to relate to such a state of mind. Most of us struggle constantly to discover the meaning of life and 'Road to Damascus' experiences are rare and, in some cases, not to be trusted.

It's not that I cannot believe those who are rock solid in their faith, it is just that I think most of us respond better to those folk for whom serenity and faith are ongoing states of mind that constantly need to be worked at. It is easy for serenity to become smugness and for faith to become complacency if they are never tested or questioned.

David Jenkins, the former Bishop of Durham, once defended his stance on Christianity to me by saying that if one's faith could not stand questioning then it was not a faith worth having.

The faiths of the people I interviewed were varied, but then I have yet to meet any two human beings who believe in precisely the same things even if they come from the same religious group.

The stories they had to tell were enriching and enlightening. Terry Waite confessed that his cell during those four years of captivity in Beirut seemed totally empty: God did not seem to be present; he somehow had to find Him within himself. Dame Cicely Saunders explained how she felt called in her nursing career to work for the relief of pain, and why she is so opposed to euthanasia.

Labour MP Frank Field, a man who worked tirelessly for the Child Poverty Action Group, was moved to tears as he recalled the way he was treated during a re-selection contest in his constituency. His unshakeable beliefs in what was right kept him going.

Some talked of how their faith had helped them overcome difficulties, and some, like gardener and countryman Geoffrey Smith, received enormous postbags from viewers who were touched by what they heard.

The series did seem to inspire viewers in offering the inspiration of men and women in the public eye, though few of them could have experienced the kind of rags-to-riches-to-rags lifestyle of novelist Susan Howatch who, having made a fortune as a writer gave up the fast cars and the high life and endowed a lectureship in theology at Cambridge University with a million pounds.

Actress Stephanie Cole's experiences are perhaps easier to relate to. Having dabbled with all kinds of beliefs she recalled the words of Carl Jung who suggested that one should go back to the faith one was born into. Stephanie did, and found what she was looking for.

No two people are alike and everyone has different spiritual requirements. In showing how some people have struggled against overpowering odds – like Emma Nicholson MP who has a hearing loss – perhaps we can find inspiration ourselves.

There's a line in the film *Shadowlands*, about the writer C.S. Lewis, in which one of his students explains why he reads so many books. His father told him, he says, that we read 'to know that we are not alone'. Hopefully the same can be said of the interviews that go to make up *Sweet Inspiration*.

# GEOFFREY SMITH

*Geoffrey Smith is everybody's idea of a Yorkshire-man, and the scenery in which he lives is a typical Yorkshire Dales landscape. I met him at his home in a quiet village high up in the Dales, outside Harrogate. We sat on a bench to talk in the tran-quillity of his garden. When he first found the high, exposed garden with its poor soil, it seemed suitable only for alpines, but now it brims with primulas, gentians, lilies, roses, rhododendrons, irises, herbs . . . a fragrant mini-Eden.*

*Geoffrey made his reputation as a gardener at Harlow Carr, the Northern Horticultural Centre's botanical gardens. And through* Gardeners' Question Time *on radio, followed by television programmes like* Mr Smith's Vegetable Garden *and* Geoffrey Smith's World of Flowers, *he became a household name.*

I have reached a stage in life now where I am contented, but there is still one thing I would like to do: to write a book about a childhood in the Yorkshire Dales – because it was a magic time.

I'm getting on a bit now, and I grew up in the Dales before machinery really came in. The doctor had a car, and the local garage proprietor had one, but there were no tractors: it was all horse work, and I love horses . . . I love animals. Although my dad wasn't a farmer, I spent my childhood on a dog-and-stick Dales farm, where the farmer's family made me welcome as if I were one of their own. They had twenty-two cows they milked, they had eighty sheep, a dozen pigs, and it was all organic and complete and interdependent. I would love to write the book to give expression to a way of life that was too good to lose.

Which is why I get upset at some *off cummed un* – some outsider – from London, and even worse *off cummed uns* from Brussels, telling Dales farmers how to make a living! These farmers have been doing it for centuries, and the Dales are as they are because they have an instinctive understanding of what is good for the land.

None of this rubbishy bagged muck, lad! You go to the top end of Swaledale and see those meadows in bloom: meadow cranesbill, the grasses, the rust hue, the colour and the scent – that's organic farming and that's organic living, which in certain parts of the Dales they still enjoy. I'd love to write about that, and to say how good it was to go to a village school, and to play in a village cricket team.

The wildlife in the garden interested me as much as the plants. As a small child, I can remember my mother being infuriated because I used to get up in the night and watch the badgers. She didn't cotton on to this until one morning when my dad went into my bedroom at half past six, which was the time he got up, and found my bed was empty: I'd got up at quarter past three to go and watch the badgers.

That was when the mystery of nature began to unravel itself for me. I can remember, about two years after that, I popped along to see the badgers after school – I went to the village school; the best foundation for any child is a village school – and all the badgers were dead, hanging over the trees. And I remember meeting the gamekeeper, and I was crying – you see, I knew these badgers, they were friends of mine; they had got used to me, they had eaten my peanut butter sandwiches . . . and somebody had killed them.

Later, the gamekeeper told my dad, 'If that lad had been big enough, I think he would have killed me.' I think I would have done. I couldn't understand why the badgers had to be killed – and all the gamekeeper had to say to me was, 'What's up, lad? They're just blankety-blank badgers!'

And that is the wrong attitude towards wildlife. You don't kill it because it's there: you love it and watch it because it's there. I may be getting on a bit now, but I am still overcome by the wonder and the joy of creation – and yet the mystery too, because you can't explain it. It's too complex, too magical, and the more I explore the magic, the more I believe.

*Geoffrey was born in a little village called Barningham, on the Pennines.*

Up under the Stang between Swaledale and Teesdale, there was a blunt-ended little dale and the village perched up about a thousand feet above sea level, on the edge of the moors.

And it is purely beautiful still. It hasn't changed – there has been no extraneous building – and whenever I want reassurance that the world really is right, underneath all the turmoil, I go back there. I do the walk along the River Greta and I inhale the quiet; it soaks in through my skin, and I see things that haven't changed in all the years I've known it: primroses still grow in the same place, the bluebell woods are still beautiful at this time of the year.

I've never taken it for granted – it's too precious not to notice, and too vulnerable. If you don't watch it, if everyone who is concerned about the countryside doesn't look after it, there will be none left. Because there is always some John waiting there to say, 'Isn't it beautiful? We'll put a factory, we'll put a house there.' It doesn't take care of itself: the farmers – no, the *whole community* has to take care of it.

I've always wanted to work outside, with the country-side. I remember one morning when I left boarding school, vowing that I would never work inside. It may seem a bit strange to think of me as a boarder. I went to boarding school on a scholarship – the biggest mistake I ever made! – but my brother had been there, and it did teach me one useful thing: it convinced me that I would never work inside. So I left and joined the Forestry Commission.

I had to get up at 5.30 in the morning to cycle to work; it took me an hour, in the early light. I remember one morning in May, when the valley was filled with that peculiar diaphanous mist; and as the sun came up, it came through the mist and sucked it up – and the valley was revealed in all that vivid greenery that you find here in the Dales. It was as if I was seeing beauty for the first time.

It made such an impression on me that I have never forgotten just how precious beautiful things are – and how vulnerable they are. I bet, on a May morning, there is still mist there, and there is still sunlight that sucks it up, and there are still four petal primroses growing in that same valley . . . and that's my reassurance.

That's why *Morning Has Broken* is one of my favourite hymns: it sums up that May morning experience, because it is an encapsulation of the natural world as I love it best.

I was in the church choir when I was a boy. My mother had a gorgeous voice, and it was on the strength of her voice that I was stuck in the choir; I reckon a jackdaw or a crow and I have a fair match! I always stood next to a lad called Ben Powell, who had a superb singing voice and used to warble away full top chords, while I used to croak quietly in the background. I masked my lack of ability behind a boy who had plenty – and he used to thump me when we got outside for making such a disgusting noise.

Although I can't sing, it gives me tremendous pleasure to hear people who can. The human voice is surely the most expressive instrument of all: you can express every emotion, much more even than on a piano or violin. When you sit and listen to a great choir, particularly if you are listening to them from somewhere like York Minster, then you can hear the true meaning of hymns.

My mum was red-haired and had a temper to match and a heart as big as a house. She could be shrieking that she was going to murder me one minute – and then cuddling me the next to make sure I didn't believe it. My dad was the gentlest man I've ever known. I never heard him raise his voice, ever. He was a professional gardener, but he never suggested a career for me. When I went into gardening he must have been bitterly disappointed, because he had spent quite a bit of money on my education. But he never questioned my decision. He taught me himself for the first six years of my apprenticeship – and he had a lot more to teach me when he was killed. But he had at least lived long enough to see me become the superintendent at Harlow Carr.

He was killed in a road accident. My mother always used to watch for him coming from work, and one day she was watching out of the window and she saw the wagon hit him. She wouldn't accept it, of course, for months and months and months. It was a hard way for a gentle man to die. But if we have any faith at all, surely we must realise that there are better things ahead for us.

My dad's favourite hymn was *The Lord's My Shepherd*. He reckoned that was the most marvellous piece of writing ever:

> *Yea, though I walk through death's dark vale,*
> *Yet will I fear none ill;*
> *For Thou art with me, and Thy rod*
> *And staff me comfort still.*

In adversity, David was, when he wrote that, wasn't he? He was in the cave with a few followers, a hunted man – and yet he could write like that. Now that really is faith, isn't it? And that was the sort of faith my dad had.

*As a child, Geoffrey was made to go to church three times on a Sunday: morning service, Sunday school and evensong.*

I rebelled, naturally, when I was old enough to make my own decisions about it. I used to think, why go to church when the sun was shining? Nature itself is the greatest cathedral, and I wanted to be out in it. I went through a phase where I avoided going to church, and I questioned my faith and argued about it.

I can remember saying to my uncle that I thought I was agnostic. He said, 'Well, that is a good thing, Geoffrey, because while you are questioning, you are believing.'

In those teenage years, I was searching around, reading about different religions, and I came to the conclusion that the people who probably had the best sympathy of all with the environment were the North American Indians and the Tibetans. They never did anything that harmed the land: they were at one with nature.

We fool ourselves, you know, in thinking that we humans are not a part of the natural world. We jolly well are, and we will be made to pay if we don't subscribe to the normal, God-given rules of the natural world. So although I kicked against religion, I came back to it, and now my church is as much a part of my life as working and everything else.

When you live in the countryside, you are brought face to face with the reality, all the time, that this couldn't have happened by accident – there is no way that this world could have happened just with a Big Bang! It's much too exact. The basis of all life is totally dependent on that green colouring in the grass, in the foliage of the trees: life couldn't exist without that.

And what about our appreciation of beauty? That is a God-given thing: our love of music, love of poetry, good literature. What point has any of that, in the frantic rush of the world of natural selection? It hasn't any place at all.

So yes, in spite of my arguing – and I occasionally do still argue with Him, believe me, and ask Him what He thinks is going on – I am still brought back to that basic belief that I have always had: that there is a God, and that there was a man called Jesus Christ, who lived and spoke words of infinite wisdom – that would make a marvellous guideline for the politicians of this world. I can't get away from it.

I was baptised a Methodist and then I went to the established Church, and I now attend the Baptist church, so I've been through a fair experimental programme. I think non-conformism is healthy – anything that breaks a pattern that is established over generations is good, surely, as long as it breaks it in a vital, creative form; I don't mean change for the sake of change. Non-conformism is still one of the great blessings of the Dales folk because there's a simplicity to it. They don't dress religion up in cant and hypocrisy and formal types of worship: it is improvised, if you like, and from the heart.

I like people. Harlow Carr was open to the public, and I'd have driven myself insane if I hadn't liked people. The sort of people I find difficult are those who are very self-opinionated. But I think everybody has a good point somewhere – though sometimes you have to search!

To a degree we make ourselves who we are, but I think in most respects we're formed by circumstances. I happen to have been lucky in that I've lived with country people, whose simplicity I understand and find totally trustworthy. If you grow up in the Dales community, you've got to (a) be an optimist and (b) like people. You're ostracised if you don't join in everything. I couldn't stand aloof and not join in the things that were going on around me.

*Geoffrey sees himself as a typical Yorkshireman . . .*

Mind, I can see good even in folks from Lancashire, so I am probably not totally typical! No, to be serious, I am a typical Yorkshireman, with an intense love and regard for the Dales. Although my dad was a Norfolk man, and way back in my ancestry there was Irish blood, which is probably why I like singing and beautiful things and poetry. I love watching folk dancing, for example, so I am in fact a complex mixture, though mostly Yorkshire, thank goodness.

I've got the Yorkshire competitiveness, too. You couldn't play cricket in Yorkshire and not be competitive. If, after the second over, you weren't looking at the ball for the blood on it, then you're not a real Yorkshireman. I've enjoyed all this because I grew up in a village where sport was an essential part of communal life. We had a super cricket team and the best crowd of lads I've ever played with. It was because everybody was playing for the team there. It wasn't a lot of people playing for their own batting average: everybody played for the team, and played aggressively. The next door village was the one to put on the carpet. You had to have them all back in their hutch quick or you didn't get noticed the next day.

When I think of all my weaknesses, where can I start? Possibly I'm not as tolerant as I should be. I have a tendency, particularly in gardening, to think my way is right; I should listen more to people.

And I'm always self-critical. I can remember being told at college by Captain Anderson, who was a lecturer in horticulture there, 'If you don't stop being a perfectionist, you'll never make a good gardener.' But now I would argue about that, because I do still search for perfection, both in writing and in gardening.

I have a temper – explosive on occasions, although it takes a lot to make me lose it. As my brother used to say, 'I can push you so far, our Geoff, and then your eyes go as cold as ice and that's when I start running.' Even though he was four years older than me. He was a god to me, of course, being four years older. But then I found his feet of clay: he couldn't play cricket as well as me – or could he?

If I could change anything that's happened in my life, I would change several acrimonious moments – there are times when I've been unkind to people; but I wouldn't change the major points in my life so far. God has never let me down: it is me that has let Him down, when I have gone pig-headed. That's my great fault: I don't stop long enough to listen. I'm a creature of impulse on so many occasions – but when it comes to Christianity, I'm not an impulsive Christian; not by any manner of means. That is more serious than mere impulse.

When I've got problems, the shortest way of solving them, I've found, is to go to a place that's quiet and talk to God about it. I have no qualms about admitting to praying about difficulties, whether they're small or big. We all come to watersheds in our faith and in our personal life, whether or not we are aware of how critical those are. Let me give an instance.

I was on my way up to Perth to a weekend course. I knew there were two choices facing me, and that I was in danger of being extremely unchristian. People sometimes imagine that if you're a Christian you don't suffer temptation, but you do indeed, believe me. You're a normal human being; there's no question about that. I knew that I was at a particular crossroads, so I did what I always do. I took the problem to God. It's the simplest way: put the onus on Him, that's my attitude; it really is as simple as that. All you've got to do is stop, and think, and go into a church, which is what I did on this occasion.

It was a church built of pink stone. When I went in, the Friends of Iona were conducting a service and they were singing a very ancient Irish hymn, *Be Thou My Vision*. I sat in there quietly and thought my problem through, and asked for advice – and the advice was simple.

I stayed right through the service, right to the end, and when I came out there was no question about what I should do and what my attitude should be; none whatsoever! It doesn't always happen like that, but on most occasions, it does.

*Be Thou My Vision* is my favourite hymn of all. The words are a counselling:

> *Be Thou my vision, O Lord of my heart,*
> *Be all else but naught to me, save that Thou art,*
> *Be Thou my best thought in the day or the night,*
> *Both waking and sleeping, Thy presence my light.*

I know I am safeguarded then. It is a sort of sigh of relief, that everything is made plain if you ask. Certainly I think that all the great decisions in life are best conducted with somebody who has the power to advise you rightly.

I pray every day – and not just at set times, although I also have my prayer time. I read a passage of the Bible each day; I've got a book that I buy in January each year that has a set Bible reading for the day. I find it brings the Bible alive and gives it an everyday meaning.

*In 1974, Geoffrey left Harlow Carr to concentrate on gardening on radio and television.*

Of course I have enjoyed enormously being on television. It is the showman in us, wanting to express our views and introduce our ideas to other people without getting talked back to! That's the magic of it, nobody answers you back on television. You can stand there and expound what you think is great philosophy and nobody shouts at you.

I've done loads of television gardening; there was *Gardeners' World*, then there was the *Mr Smith's* series. I got into television by falling on a producer's head. He had come up to interview three people that Harlow Carr had suggested as possible presenters. I could see this man, walking about the garden like a lost sheep, because I was high up, lopping an oak tree. He hadn't seen me, but when I came down the rope, he heard a thud and turned round – and there I was, like Mephistopheles coming out of the undergrowth!

I frightened him, I really did, so I took him up to the house that I lived in, in the corner of the garden, and gave him tea and scones – and at the end of our conversation, he said: 'Would you like to do television?' And I said, 'Yes, anything for a new experience.' And he said, 'Well, come down and do ten minutes on michaelmas daisies. Can you raise enough enthusiasm to do ten minutes' exciting television on michaelmas daisies?' He obviously thought it would be quite a challenge. But you see, I took the story of this species right back to the dawn of time – and it went down very well.

The next one I did was on rock gardens. I took the cream of alpines with me, and I remember Percy Thrower, who was a splendid television man – I don't think there's ever been anyone quite like Percy: he had that curious magic that people loved – I can remember him saying, because it was all live in those days, 'For goodness' sake, don't dry up, Geoff, because I don't know any of their names!' because they were all fairly rare alpines. Oh, yes, I enjoyed it.

But I'm doing less television now. I'm backing out of it because, really, after *World of Flowers*, which was the most exciting gardening television you could possibly imagine (fancy tracing peonies back to their origins and pelargonias back to South Africa!), to come back to 'you sows your broad beans under the waxing moon', and 'you sows your runner beans on this moon', and 'you dung the ground and the answer's in the soil' – and that sort of thing; I couldn't go back to that.

And I'm not star-struck about television. I didn't come into television until fairly late in life, so I was mature enough to evaluate it and not believe the sort of image of me that the television projects, which the public then recaptures and projects back. I don't believe the public image of myself, except with a tongue in my cheek.

I know my own fallibility. It would have been very easy to become self-important; I could feel it beginning to intrude, expecting doors to be opened for me. But I know I was no better gardener because I was on television than I was before I went on! I am a good gardener now, and I always have been, but that's because I have learned my profession; the real satisfaction is not being on television but in growing plants.

If you could have the Yorkshire Dales on your doorstep and you could say, 'Well, on Saturday, I'm going to drop off at Greta Bridge, and I'm going to walk that length of the Greta and just let the quiet serenity of springtime soak into my blood,' would you change all that to live out of a suitcase – just to work on television? No, I'll settle for what I've got.

*In 1988, Geoffrey was rushed into hospital for an emergency operation.*

I walked very close to death six years ago, with my appendix. I would have died but for Marjorie, God bless her. Forty years I've been married to that woman, and I still appreciate her more than I did when I started.

She overruled me: I had insisted that she didn't ring for the doctor, saying, 'It's only your cooking, lass' – she's a splendid cook! – but she gave me until the evening and then called the doctor. And by then I was almost past caring, because the appendix had burst and turned gangrenous.

That episode concentrated my mind and made me appreciate what marvellous people nurses are. One in particular, Sister Worth, insisted that I didn't die; she was quite adamant about it. And I'm grateful for a Nigerian surgeon who wasn't frightened to put the knife in; if he hadn't operated straight away to take the appendix out, without waiting for confirmation of this, that and the other, I wouldn't have survived.

About three days after the operation – apparently that's when infection builds up and attacks, when you're at your lowest ebb – they rang Marjorie up and said that I would have to be rushed down to emergency again, that it was a serious business.

But I had a sensation of being buoyed up. I didn't know my wife and family and the church were praying for me, but I had the sense of being lifted up. Don't you ever kid yourself or ever underestimate the power of prayer. I'm a rough Dalesman, and not easily conned, but prayer has an immense power, both of healing and sustaining – and release, if you like, and reassurance.

Yes, I am a great believer in it. And not the prayer wheel of the Tibetans, the *om mani padme hom*, although I've got a lot of time for the religion of the Tibetans and the religion of the North American Indians. I happen to think they're misguided: I happen to think that Christianity is *the* true way. But they believe in the power of prayer, and so do I as a Christian. Very much so.

I wouldn't have slipped away willingly, because I would have left so much that I loved behind. But it would have been very easy. Surely I'm a poor sort of Christian if I don't anticipate that death is the last great adventure. If

I have believed all my life in a God that *isn't*, then I'm the most deluded of people.

Mind, let me tell you something. There's a little bit on that walk up the Greta where, if I don't want to walk the whole length, I would branch off at Gill Beck. And there's a little dale there, where there are primroses covering a bankside at this time of year, and silver birch and hazel, and there's a wee valley there that I'm sure nobody goes to except me. And when the time comes for me to depart this world, I would like it to be abrupt and I'd like it to be in a place that's beautiful, because then there wouldn't be such a shock of change! And that little valley – well, if paradise is any better, I can't wait to get there, because it is singularly beautiful, it really is.

My ideal day would go like this. If I could stop the world going round the seasons, I'd stop them at the last week in May, the first week in June. And I would spend the whole of that time roaming from the meeting of the waters, following that gorgeous river, the Greta, up to Rudderford Bridge, the ford of the oxen. And then I would cut out of the fertile valley and up on to the tops; I'd walk the Badger Way across the moors, and then I would come down on the old green Lonning, the green road that the Romans knew, into Newsham; I would walk on to Ravensworth and the little pub on the village green, and I would have a steak and kidney pie and pint of beer . . . and I would say: 'That is perfect.'

The sun would shine, the birds would sing, there would be primroses and bluebells and that peace that really embraces the countryside at this time of the year, because bird song and bee noise and the tone of water only serve to emphasise the perennial quiet of places like that.

If I didn't live in a situation like this I would probably fade away in a week. It's got everything I want here: the quiet and the countryside around me. I was a countryman before I was a gardener.

I've just bought a field of two and a half acres that has got a beck and gorse bushes – and I'm going to fill it with wild flowers, and I'm going to sit there.

The farmer who bid for the same field said, 'What are you going to do with it, Geoff?'

I said, 'I'm going to sit and look at it.'

And he looked at me and said, 'You're daft, you know!'

And I said, 'It's a very, very splendid form of madness, though.' Isn't it?

## Be Thou My Vision

Be Thou my vision, O Lord of my heart,
Be all else but naught to me, save that Thou art;
Be thou my best thought in the day and the night,
Both waking and sleeping, Thy presence my light.

Be Thou my wisdom, be Thou my true word,
Be Thou ever with me, and I with Thee, Lord;
Be Thou my great Father, and I Thy true son;
Be Thou in me dwelling, and I with Thee one.

Riches I heed not, nor man's empty praise:
Be Thou mine inheritance now and always;
Be Thou and Thou only the first in my heart;
O Sovereign of heaven, my treasure Thou art.

High King of heaven, Thou heaven's bright Sun,
O grant me its joys after vict'ry is won;
Great Heart of my own heart, whatever befall,
Still be Thou my vision, O Ruler of all.

*Irish, eighth century*

# FRANK FIELD

*Labour MP Frank Field's flat is only a brisk walk away from the House of Commons. We talk together in his living room. Quietly distinguished and artistic, it is furnished like a gentleman's study and lined to the ceiling with books, mostly large and serious volumes on philosophy and religion. It is a scholarly but inviting room, flooded with natural light from the balcony: clearly a good place to think and reflect – something that Frank does every day. He seems to take nothing for granted but mulls over his beliefs and ideas with scrupulous, even painful, honesty.*

*I am surprised at first by his nervousness – surely politicians are used to interviews – but Frank isn't doing a politician's performance, giving ready-made answers. He is saying what he is feeling right now, and that's always risky . . .*

I was born in north London. I would have been born in Chiswick, where I grew up, but air-raids decided that my mother should go to north London, and that's where I was born.

My mother was a great influence on all of us, as children, but purely through her gentleness. She always led us by example: there was no preaching. And though she had a very difficult marriage, none of us – my brothers nor I – realised till much later just how tough she must have found it. From her, we had enormous security.

I learned there why the family is so important: it is the only place where we can experience some – not all, but some – decisions being made on the basis of love. Not only is the family clearly what God deems as the way we should be raised, but it's teaching us something about the

Kingdom, where that principle of love will operate. Once we get outside the family we can sometimes re-experience that, but usually we have to fall back on a man-made system of fairness, of equity. But without that secure background of family love, I don't think we can be that good even at the man-made justice. Therefore I attach a great deal of importance to the upbringing I had from my mother.

My father was a pretty horrendous figure for me, and I think for my brothers as well. He didn't like us, that's the short of it. He was only happy when we'd grown up and left home. I had no real relationship with my father. That's the sadness of it all. One of the great joys is seeing dads behaving like dads, rather than in the monstrous way that he behaved. There was a great deal of tension – and he was pretty brutal.

I remember vividly the last time that he tried to attack me, when I was fifteen. I took the hammer away and said, 'Next time, I'll use that on you.' He never tried that again – and that taught me quite a lot about bullying. Something that people in politics often fail to understand is that you have to treat different people in different ways. If you want to do things with me, you only have to be nice to me and I'll do it straight away. If you try and bully me, then all that old resistance that I learned from childhood comes to the fore; and I can well look after myself in those circumstances.

My father worked as a labourer in a factory, Morgan's Crucible, in Battersea. He took the job in the recession because his own father was a drunk and he was the eldest son, and he therefore felt he had the responsibility to bring a wage packet home. He didn't marry until all his brothers and sisters had left home – so there's a good side to him as well. And although he had won scholarships, he hadn't been able to take them up; so it was obviously hard for him to see his sons not working hard or making the most of their scholarships.

If you were amongst the labouring classes at Morgan's, when you retired, you were allowed to buy yourself a present worth a pound a year for each year that you had worked there. And so my father went off to – I think it was Arding and Hobbs, at Clapham Junction – to buy a canteen of cutlery. As he had worked at Morgan's for forty-eight years, he submitted a bill to them for exactly £48. And they sent him back a bill for £10!

That was when the scales fell from his eyes. Because he was a working-class Tory, he had always believed in hierarchy, believed in deference, believed that some people should rule, believed that these people had special skills and values which the rest of us didn't have. But they couldn't even bother to get that right, about how long he had worked there. It radicalised him late in life. It's like the deadliest line in *Doctor Zhivago*, where the awful old Bolsheviks have destroyed Lara, and Zhivago recalls, 'They didn't even know where they did it.' It's that sort of carelessness: the opposite of what hierarchy is supposed to be, when they preach about the people at the top having duties and responsibilities as well as rights.

My father had to argue, to go through the degrading process of asking them to check their records, so that they could see they shouldn't have sent their bill. That incident also radicalised me – not only about the frailty of human nature, but also about how poles apart this was from how every individual ought to be treated. Instead of the indiscriminate love of God, here's the rotten old job we do as human beings!

It was against this sort of background that we grew up. Not one with lots of money; we were conscious that pennies counted, though we never went without. How scaled down our values were, our demands were – our *needs* were, then. It's very difficult to talk about living standards all those years ago, and make comparisons between whether one was poorer then or now. The pressures on parents today, to buy all these things for Christmas and so on . . . we didn't have that. And I think practically everybody fed better then. The relative price of food has risen enormously, and therefore people on lower incomes now have that much less to spend on food.

*The Field family went to church every Sunday.*

It was a great treat for me. I was taken to this wonderful, huge building (which, I only discovered a few years ago, was built by Pearson, my favourite Victorian architect). It was very high church, so there was mystery, there was music, there was darkness, there was light, there were lofty dark spaces as well as friendliness – beautiful contrasting things and beautiful sounds, all encapsulated in that building.

It taught me a great lesson, that not everything can be put over in nice neat little sentences. Aneurin Bevan once said (and if he didn't say it, he would have said it had he thought of it!) that 'listening to the Prime Minister Neville Chamberlain was like a trip round Woolworth's: everything in place, and nothing over sixpence'. That early experience in church taught me that we don't always have a language that can adequately describe the really important things in life. We stretch and we grope . . . but there are lots of things in this world greater than us individuals, however clever and important we may think we are.

As I was in the choir, it was twice on Sundays to church for me. And there was choir practice as well; I always enjoyed all that. There were a group of us, and we were taken on treats and given various other bribes to keep us together – it showed a really good understanding of human nature, recognising that self-interest has to be satisfied!

I think singing hymns is important because, so lacking in confidence is the Church, it has very largely given up teaching us and therefore it is through hymns that we get a lot of our religion now. That's the way that the 'rumour of God' is handed on in our society.

It's only recently that I've discovered there's such a thing as Advent, the beginning of the year and the promise that things could be made anew. It emphasises, of course, how thick I am, that I've only come to Advent quite late in life when clearly it has been around for two thousand years! But I now love Advent more than any other season of the year. For me, this discovery is important, not only because of the beauty of the hymns and the carols, but because of the message, and that is: it's a new beginning, all the time. And because we can't manage to remember that every day, Advent is put into one part of the year – to remind us that, whenever we want it, there can be a new beginning.

*Frank read Economics at the University of Hull. But his interest in politics was kindled while he was still at his London grammar school, St Clement Danes.*

We had a really good sixth form, where we were all expected to get through exams and win scholarships. We read the *Listener* then, the magazine the BBC has now shut down. It took us out into the big world: the world of geography and the world of ideas. It was during those discussions that a lot of us became interested in politics, not in the party sense but in the sense of wanting to know what was going on.

And with all the arrogance of youth, one thought one should do something about it, and *could* do something about it. I'm a lot less sure about what one can do about things now than I was then! If, back in the sixth form, I'd had the doubt I now have about human nature and about our ability to govern and influence affairs, I probably wouldn't have chosen the sort of career I've had!

I'm a great struggler with most of my beliefs and ideas, and my faith is no different from that. I am not full of certainties. Indeed, being questioned now about my faith has sent me into a spin – today's spin! – about whether it is all true. That's the big question really: is it just a cop-out that we believe, or is there something really basic there, which is much bigger and more important than all of us?

I don't have that experience that some people have,

that wonderful conversion experience of *knowing* God is there. I don't have that gift; I envy them for having it. My faith is built up on a series of balances: just on probability it does seem more likely to be true. Also, through music one gets some idea that there is something beyond this life, something much more wonderful than what we experience here.

But it is a struggle. Most days I doubt – and then I end the day thinking, well, my faith does help to make sense of it all.

*Frank was appointed Director of the Child Poverty Action Group in 1968, and ran it till 1979, when he was elected Labour MP for Birkenhead. But his concern with alleviating poverty continued, both in the House of Commons and as Director of the Low Pay Unit (1974–80).*

Well, it may be that people say I understand poverty better than anybody else in Parliament, but I don't think it's true. I certainly don't understand poverty nearly as well as those who are on the receiving end of it. My job is to articulate in the House of Commons some of the big issues that confront the country, but I want to get away from the feeling that somehow poverty is so damned complicated that only a few people can possibly understand it.

My experience of trying to grapple with any topic – whether it's Bosnia, whether it's nuclear testing, whatever topic you take – is that on the level of detail it is immensely complicated. And poverty is no more complicated than any of these other topics. But at a moral level, poverty raises a pretty simple question: how are we sharing both our country's and the world's resources? *Is it fair?*

If we were to be struck down now, and held accountable for our use of time and resources, could we justify what is actually going on in Britain? And in the world today? I think the answer to that is 'no'. So while it's true to say that the issue of poverty is complicated in some senses, with all those damn regulations and so on, it is essentially a moral issue – and we confront the Second Commandment: self-love is immensely important, but we also have the job of loving our neighbours as ourselves. In this country, when you see the extremes of rich and poor – people sleeping on the streets! – it is clearly a commandment which we fail to live up to, me included.

The awful paradox that I have to accept, of course, is that poverty has given me a career. I do carry that around with me, the knowledge that I've done well out of it; but that is a spur to keep me going, to try and get reforms through that benefit other people too.

You ask me whether I am a realist or an idealist. It's not a question of seeing life as either one or the other: I think one has to be both. I think you have got to be a realist in the sense that you have to take into account what human nature is like, to recognise human limitations: for example the way our loyalties tend to be primarily to our family and to our street, and then maybe to our town and to our country. As we get further and further away from ourselves, our concern for others gets weaker. But I think we need to balance that self-interest with idealism, with altruism, which is also a part of human nature, so that we're not just inward-looking but also looking out. Heresy is not people peddling lies: heresy comes when you peddle one truth at the expense of all other truths.

Therefore I think our conversation with Mrs Thatcher ought to have been different: not to have laughed at her, not to have dismissed her, but to have said, 'You are absolutely right to emphasise self-interest. But if we only do that, then we are peddling a heresy: we are ignoring the other side of human nature, which *can* be altruistic – and that altruism is necessary, if we're not just to have a scramble of the rich taking everything.' And I think that's an appeal that we could make, and that we ought to have made, fifteen years ago.

The Gospels have a message – of the power of redemption to turn us from just self-interest towards that ideal of indiscriminate love. It is through worship and through the Church that we, as a community of failures, are helped in this respect. And for the particularly frail, like me, the *beauty* of worship is very important, because offering beauty is a tangible way, a physical way, of trying – childlike – to offer up to God our very best.

I'm a straight up and down Christian in that I believe in God, a personal God, a God that became man, who lived amongst us, and therefore attaches tremendous importance to what goes on in this world. For me, it's not a privatised religion: my God is one who was actually killed and rose again, and therefore holds out that promise of resurrection to us.

That's the framework of my belief – but most days are filled with doubt; I wonder whether what I say I believe is true. Or is it just something which we've hooked on to because it's more convenient than to face the alternative, which is that there's nothing for any of us once we die? That doubting that I experience, that struggling, is best summed up for me by R S Thomas, our best poet this century. He wrote about a man 'testing his faith/On emptiness, nailing his questions/One by one to an untenanted cross'. I test my questions on emptiness all the time. It's one of the extraordinary things about prayer, isn't it, that – by definition – God knows what you are going to say? And you are having a conversation with a person that doesn't reply to you! At least not directly. It's a very strange sort of conversation.

Joan of Arc had a good reply, when one of the clever bishops said to her, 'All these voices are in your mind, aren't they?' She said, 'Of course they are, how else do you think God talks to us?'

At present I'm trying to write my first biography – of George Bell, a great bishop in the 1930s, and I can't make sense of him . . . so I am having *two* conversations with people, neither of whom answer the questions I pose to them!

*Frank joined the Labour Party because he was so
impressed by the principled stand taken by Hugh
Gaitskill challenging the racism implicit in the
original Commonwealth immigration policies.*

I admired the way that he took on a topic about which
every clever politician said, 'Don't touch this, play this
one cool.' Of all the things I most loathe in political
activity, the worst is playing the racist card. For me, it's
a cardinal point.

There is a very active National Front group in Birkenhead. I get on pretty hotly with them; although it's our
duty to try and understand why people do it – partly
because of lack of work and partly because there is a very
nasty side to human nature, which we all share. But that
bullying, that kicking people below one, is pretty evident
in their activities. And the whole way that we've accepted,
in this country, that large numbers of families live in fear of
being burned out by these thugs – it is just unacceptable.

I am still very proud of my Englishness. I think I am in
the minority in Birkenhead: most of the rest of the town
came from Scotland, Ireland and Wales to work at the
shipyard – when we had one. But despite our differences,
I think that we're probably very similar in the aspirations
that we hold.

*The media repeatedly sketches Frank as a politician
with an unusual degree of integrity and courage, but
an ascetic and a loner.*

I was dreading that you'd ask me if I were lonely – please
don't make me out to be, as some people do, or I will get
a huge postbag of letters to me saying, 'You needn't be
lonely, I'm here!'

I think one does need space. I enjoy being on my
own, though I like the company of other people as
well. Certainly there's an ascetic side to me, and that's
the one that is regularly presented in the media because
that's the easiest one to do. But it is exaggerated. When

there was a profile of me that said I didn't drink, the Dean of Peterhouse at Cambridge said he was going to reply, saying, 'The last time Frank Field was here, the Master thought we ought to lock the cellar doors because so much wine was being consumed!' There are good things in life and I think one should share in them, but also spread them around.

I don't like the idea that some people have of post-poning gratification in this life, putting on one side all the enjoyable things in the belief that we'll have them at some future time. Nor is that part of the Christian religion. The Bible is very clear on this. The Second Commandment says, 'We should love our neighbours *as ourselves*.' Self-love is incredibly important; you can't live a proper life without realising that. All we are asked to do is to make sure we love other people as best we can, as we would love ourselves. We actually need our gratification here and now, on our journey, though we also need to spread it around, so that more of us have it rather than less of us. But there is, I think, the Judgement Day, when we will be held accountable.

If you want to say something nice about somebody, you say they are courageous; if you want to rubbish them you say they are obstinate. These are flipsides of the same quality. The crucial thing is the balance you strike. If somebody practises courage to such an extreme that it becomes mere obstinacy on their part, how do you judge that?

And, as well as trying to keep hold of your ideals, you also have the job of being accepted by other people, being part of a group or party. All these things have to be balanced, one against the other. I wish I could keep this particular balance better. I mean, I'm viewed in the House of Commons as not being a team player, as an outsider – but I long to be an insider! They've got the message wrong, totally.

I suppose they have misread it partly because we politicians are very busy and therefore we depend on you, in the media, to tell us what we think. And if one is then dubbed an 'outsider', a 'maverick', an 'oddball', even by those journalists who are paid to think about the political process, then any combination that one might be able to make is very quickly undermined by those sorts of comments. It's a vicious circle. Because you don't really have to take seriously, do you, what a maverick says, or an oddball says?

But you might take seriously politicians who are deadly earnest about their party winning, and winning not because they think their ideas are necessary, and they want to put them forward in the best possible way to the country, but because they want to be in power.

I now recognise, in a way I never thought I would do, that power does corrupt. And the nicest people – and some of the cabinet are very nice people – those very nice people behave differently if they think they are always going to win and never going to lose. So, for the sake of the country now, for the health of our democracy, I think it's crucially important that we in the Labour Party get our act together so that, on polling day, we can actually win.

Is it possible that power has corrupted me too?

Well, it may have done . . . who knows the real truth about that? Freud said that none of us really knows ourselves. I hope it's not true, that power has corrupted me. But when we are all lined up there, on the last dreadful Day of Judgement, as the Prayer Book says, you may be able to say, 'I was right in putting that question to you. It was a real warning.'

Our activity here in this life is, partly, about how we use our talents. We are here to work: it's a very, very important part of our existence. Not only do I love the poetry of George Herbert, but some of his poems are set as hymns, and one of these, *Teach Me, My God and King*, emphasises the importance of making our 'drudgery divine'. It is about us replenishing the world through work, about us participating in the re-creation here, as agents of God.

Therefore, for me, one of the appalling things about our society is that there are three, four million people who would like work, but are denied the opportunity to work. And there is no urgency about trying to find ways of making sure they have that opportunity. We have deliberately decided, in this country, to exclude large numbers of people from work! They are denied that possibility of doing what they are here for, of participating in God's creation. Part of my own failure is the failure to get over certain issues like this, moving the country back again to full employment, with the urgency I think they deserve.

Failure is written large all across me. I went into the House of Commons to be part of a winning side, to bring forward certain changes. But every time we've faced the electorate, they've rollocked us round the ears! You couldn't have a bigger failure than that. And I have contributed to that failure: I've failed to be influential enough to help get the Labour Party into a position to win.

*During the 1980s Frank struggled against de-selection as MP for Birkenhead.*

Without the ability to be alone I would never have survived the re-selection battles.

At one point it was really bad in the constituency, with a small group of people deciding that they were going to drive me out. I found it an extraordinary experience having thirty or forty people *hate* one that much, wanting to destroy one. I still find it both difficult to talk about and difficult to explain, that a group of what I would have thought were quite decent people could so hate somebody that their whole effort was to destroy them.

At the height of all that, I would do what I had to do and wanted to do in my constituency on Fridays and Saturdays – but then I would want to get out. I felt an extraordinary feeling there of that hate, so I would get the first train back to London on Sunday mornings. The train journey would take five or six hours, and I knew I could have total quietness for that time with nobody talking, nothing. And that was the period I used to get myself ready for the next week, for the fight.

I would stand there while accusations would be made against me. And since it is part of human nature that one gets things wrong some of the time, I was beginning to wonder whether some of those accusations couldn't be right. You can't keep on getting up and saying, 'That is untrue! Why is that presented like that? Why has that been distorted?' without eventually beginning to doubt yourself, even though you knew the accusations were false. I'm agitated even talking about that experience; I haven't talked about it for years.

It was the period in my life that most destabilised me – and which I found most puzzling, because there were a lot of people who participated in this campaign in whom one could see really good qualities. And yet what I thought of the campaign was that it was – and it's a word I don't often use – it was evil.

It taught me an enormous amount about how complicated human nature is. And there was also this 'game with mirrors': how did they see me, that they wanted to participate in what they obviously felt was a very righteous activity? And what part did I have, either as the lightning conductor, or as the initiator, in these acts which I think were evil?

That's all behind me now, thank goodness. But it's quite interesting how Providence works. Given the way I survived against my father, it was almost as though I had been, from birth, on a Duke of Edinburgh Outward Bound scheme on how to survive in these circumstances.

And I survived. But it's obviously changed me. What it taught me about myself was how very near I was to going under. There was one Friday – the party meeting was on a Friday – when, for the first time, I vomited. I thought, 'Do I go through with this?' And then I thought, 'If I don't, I'll run for ever.'

Do I forgive? The crucial thing is to forget. What one does remember are those people that stood by you, the people who could see and reached out. I was never alone in the constituency, they knew what was going on. There was always wonderful eye contact, or people telling me, 'Don't worry, whenever you want us, we're here.' Physically reassuring me – actually holding me, some people. And in the House of Commons, when the big enquiry was going on, Clare Short took the trouble to read every single piece of paper that was submitted. She just said, 'We are not going to tolerate this bullying.' So as well as the grim side, you learn the terrific side about people and their ability to help, their leaps of imagination.

*Does Frank believe in heaven?*

I believe that there is something more than just this world – though I might struggle with the idea. To say, 'I believe in *heaven*' is difficult because it means using a language we've had from childhood, and I suppose we believe, as we grow up, that we should put aside these childish things. But the older I get, the more I see how complicated our childhood thoughts were and how wonderful childhood language is for summing up these complicated ideas. Although a phrase like 'believing in heaven' slightly jars with me, everybody knows what it means – so why not use it? Don't let's try and think of another phrase which just confuses people. Yes, I do believe in heaven.

I've no idea what will happen after death. But as a Christian I believe there is a Second Coming, that there is an end to history, that the curtain does come down, and that though none of us will be doing curtain calls, we will be accountable – not merely for our own talents but collectively for what we've done with our stewardship in this world. And we sum that idea up in these posh phrases – the eschatological view of the world, and so on – but it just means that there is a Second Coming, that there's an end to it all, and then the judgement follows.

But am I confident that it is like this, and that I will pass the test? Again I'm a sort of jelly. I'm confident and not confident. Part of me tells me it's true: how can you make sense of life without it? And part of me thinks, well, maybe it is all just an accident. So, right up to the very end, I shall be wondering, hoping, trusting . . . But I believe that there is purpose in being here, other than just being here. And that there is an afterlife – or heaven, or whatever phrase one wants to use.

I think that this sense of there being an end is important not only in giving direction to our life, but in giving it immediacy. The Prayer Book instructs us 'to live this day as if it were our last'. Now it's impossible to do that, but it's very important to try and do it – not to leave arguments unfinished, friendships broken and so on, because there may not be that next day to complete these important tasks. I don't want to make it sound easy (as Dean Inge once said, 'Jesus tells us to forgive, but we can't, can we?'). I know it's a jolly hard storyline to follow. But trying to live each day as if it were our last is an important way of giving shape to one's life, not wasting one's time, and being accountable for our talents.

And we are not here to be comfortable, we're not here to be smug or self-satisfied. We are here as frail human beings, with the hope of something much more important than our human frailty at the end of it all.


## Teach Me, My God and King

Teach me, my God and King,
In all things Thee to see,
And what I do in anything,
To do it as for Thee.

A man that looks on glass
On it may stay his eye;
Or if he pleaseth, through it pass,
And then the heaven espy.

All may of thee partake:
Nothing can be so mean,
Which with this tincture, 'For Thy sake',
Will not grow bright and clean.

A servant with this clause
Makes drudgery divine;
Who sweeps a room, as for Thy laws,
Makes that and the action fine.

This is the famous stone
That turneth all to gold;
For that which God doth touch and own
Cannot for less be told.

*George Herbert (1593–1633)*

# TERRY WAITE

*Terry Waite has recently moved to a cottage in a traditional Suffolk village – the sort so peaceful and timeless it still has no street lights. Terry's home reflects this simplicity and serenity, with its centuries-old wooden beams and its white-painted walls. Most important of all, it has a separate annexe in the garden for him to use as a solitary writing room.*

*Writing is now among Terry's favourite pursuits. His autobiography was a best-seller, and he is now working on a second book. After the final hostage rescue mission that went so terribly wrong – despite the many successful rescues before – and his bitter-sweet return from captivity in 1991, Terry has cut down dramatically on his travelling.*

*Instead he lives quietly, enjoying the very English delights of village life: a chat with a neighbour, a walk across the green for a pint, family gatherings, a potter around the garden – and hours and hours of thinking, reading and writing.*

Suffolk and Norfolk have a reputation for clergy who were independent of mind – and sometimes a little cussed. There's a wonderful story, which I believe to be true, of an unfortunate woman who brought her daughter to be baptised. At the appropriate point in the service, the clergyman said:

'Name this child!'

The lady replied, timidly, 'Lucy, sir.'

'Name this child!' he demanded again.

'Lucy, sir,' she repeated, anxiously.

'Lucifer?' he said. 'No name for a boy! I shall call him "John".'

And so Lucy was baptised John. It's a wonderful
story.

*Terry Waite was born in the village of Bollington,*
*Cheshire, the son of the local policeman.*

What gave me a taste for travel was, I think, being
brought up in a village and wondering what lay beyond
its boundaries. I was very curious to know where the river
led to: I would go down to the River Bollin and look at
it, and wonder where it started and where it finished. I
learned about maps, and saved up enough money, by
delivering newspapers, to get my first bicycle.

I had quite an argument with my father about the
bicycle because he said, 'You'd be better off with butterfly
handlebars.'

I said, 'No, I want real racing handlebars.' You know,
the ones that go all the way down. I got them eventually.

After that I started to cycle all over Cheshire. One of my
first journeys was to Chester. It's a wonderful old building,
the old sandstone cathedral in Chester and I would walk
around its walls. Then I'd cycle over into Derbyshire,
over the Cat 'n' Fiddle into Buxton. Gradually I began
to expand my horizons.

One looks back, of course, at the happy times of
childhood. But I think when I had more opportunity,
as I did have in the years of captivity in Beirut, to make
a more detailed analysis and reflection, I have to say it
was both happy and unhappy.

One was acutely conscious of, somehow, being alone. I
think part of the reason, as I look back on it now, is that
in a small village, being the son of the village policeman
meant one was subject to quite a lot of scrutiny. You are
hemmed in. It was a goldfish bowl-like existence, rather
like that faced by some children of well-known people.
Now, many of these children can escape – can get out
of the way, so to speak. But you can't get out of the
way in a village. Everybody knows you, so you're a bit
circumscribed.

There was a time when one felt it would be nice to be able to join in everything fully and freely, and yet one couldn't, in some of the escapades, because [of my father being the policeman]. It's probably one of the factors that shaped me.

As it was, I fell foul of him on a number of occasions. Sometimes I think, looking back, I was probably a little bit harshly dealt with. On one occasion, I remember it very well, on Bonfire Night, November the fifth – someone put a firework through the letterbox of a man named John Snowball. A daft thing to do.

Poor old John Snowball lived in a thatched cottage, so it was a particularly crazy thing – but kids do that sort of thing sometimes. I hadn't done it; I wasn't even there when it happened. But when the whole gang ran away through the village, I saw them running and joined them. I didn't know what they were running for, I just joined in the fun, as children will. And went home.

When my father came in – the incident had, of course, been reported to him – I was subjected to a pretty intensive interrogation. And it's interesting about that sort of thing when you're a child: you begin to think, because the interrogation is so intense, that you probably have done something wrong. It's a curious phenomenon. You begin to believe that you were actually there, almost. So there was that sort of difficulty about childhood: there was that degree of intensity and that degree of feeling in one, which were always restricted in some way.

My mother is still alive – in her eighties now. If I have a picture of my mother during my childhood, it is of her at Christmas time. Living in the countryside, in a village surrounded by farms, we'd be given a goose or a chicken for Christmas. Nowadays chicken has become such a popular food, you don't think anything of it, but in those days we only ate chicken once a year. To see a chicken at Christmas time made you think, 'Goodness me, this is a remarkable treat.'

I see my mother there, surrounded by goose feathers or chicken feathers – because we had to pluck and clean the things ourselves, of course. She was a great cook and still is – that was *her*. She centred herself very much on the home. It seems very old fashioned now, of course, a very old fashioned upbringing.

My mother came from a churchgoing family and is still a regular churchgoer. I don't ever remember my father setting foot in church – except when he was married: that was about the only time. He had, one might say, an instinctive belief. But on a Sunday evening at home, he would sit in front of the fire and sing hymns. And certainly he encouraged me to go.

I joined the choir, and it was actually the choir that kept me in the church. I went Sunday by Sunday, mostly on Sunday evenings. I hardly ever went on Sunday mornings because of delivering newspapers, to save money for my bike.

The church was only a corrugated iron structure, because we were part of the parish at Wilmslow, Cheshire, and this was just a daughter church. We used to call the place a 'tin tabernacle', and when it rained . . . ! Years later, in Africa, we lived in a house which also had a corrugated iron roof, and I remembered my early days in church when the rain came pelting down and you couldn't hear any of the service.

But I remember the old tunes. If I conjure up a picture of childhood, it's in this little country church with, probably, not a clergyman reading the service but a lay reader, a very small choir, a small congregation, and the smell of pitch pine from the pews. I always remember that distinctive smell – which I can still smell today – of pitch pine and old hymn books, and the singing of one of the old, old hymns.

Singing in the evening, when the sun is setting, a hymn that captures something of the indescribable essence of faith – which is caught, for me, not so much in the words

but somewhere in the melody – that's one of the great thing
about hymns, that the melodies stir up so many evocative
memories.

*After National Service, in 1958 Terry joined the*
*Church Army, an organisation linked to the Church*
*of England that is made up of lay people doing*
*social welfare work.*

When I was eighteen I wasn't sure which direction I
wanted to go in life. People were suggesting to me
that I might consider studying for a full-time ministry,
but that never appealed to me somehow. I didn't want
to do that.

I still don't think that my vocation lay in being ordained
into the ministry. I don't think I would be able to settle
for the type of pastoral ministry that's required of those
who are ordained. Possibly I don't want to be too
confined in a role. I think if you are ordained and
you become a clergyman, you are obliged to live out
that role as fully as you can – and part of the obligation,
I think, is to maintain a sort of tradition, to hand it
on. And though I think tradition is important, I don't
think it's my role. I like to be able to explore, to be
progressive. It's not really a lack of certainty – except
in that there are few certainties in life; very, very few
certainties. But I like to have the freedom to explore
in a way that, perhaps, I wouldn't have had if I'd been
ordained.

So I went into the army [to do National Service] – but
was discharged fairly promptly, because I couldn't wear
the battledress without some irritation: the khaki dye
didn't do me any good. When I was in hospital with
that, I came across an advertisement in a newspaper for
the Church Army. They did a great deal of social welfare
work in those days.

I went to see a local Church Army officer, and I
was very taken both by the personality of the man
and by the work he was doing. Really, he was simply

assisting people in their everyday lives and with their everyday problems. What didn't appeal to me was the name, 'Church Army'. Although, of course, military images are used in the Bible, I didn't care for a military image being associated with the Church; nor what that conveyed in terms of its Victorian hangover. But I felt that what it did was absolutely admirable – and what it still does is absolutely admirable. And so I joined.

For many years, my wife Frances and I lived and worked overseas. When we were quite young and our children were only small, we went off to live and work in Africa. I was advisor to the first African archbishop, and largely responsible for the training development of clergy and senior lay people in Africa.

It was very, very interesting; a remarkable experience. After my colleagues and I had got a whole programme of training going, right at the end, Uganda began to collapse. There was a coup, Amin came to power, and the Church was put through the most dreadful, difficult days. The bishops, clergy, lay people in that country – they were remarkable people, remarkably strong in their faith, and cheerful in the most adverse circumstances.

There are a lot of people who impressed me during those years, but there is one person who stands out in my life: Desmond Tutu. I got to know Desmond very well, first of all before he was a bishop and then later on when he became the first black African archbishop in South Africa. I think he impressed me because I saw what enormous pressures a black African leader had to face in those days of change.

I remember when Desmond was with the South African Council of Churches. It appeared as though there was a real attempt by some people to discredit the man and to discredit the Council. I thought to myself, 'How does he withstand these attacks on his character, these attacks on his family, this constant bombardment, constant vilification by the press and others?'

He took it with such good humour. It affected him, of course, it would affect anybody, but he took it with such calm serenity – and the reason he was able to do that was, in my opinion, because of the deep core of faith in him and the real trust, which impressed me enormously. A very great man.

Our next overseas posting was in Italy. I was seconded for a period of work for the Roman Catholic Church, helping the development of preventative health programmes. Not that I am in any way a medical specialist, but I did know something about organisation, about development and about development education.

Later on, when Robert Runcie was appointed Archbishop of Canterbury, he was looking for someone who had international experience to help him in his role as *primus inter pares* – 'first among equals' – of the archbishops of the Anglican communion. Someone who could arrange his visits, travel with him, brief him on matters concerning the Church overseas. And that's how it came my way.

The job had the remarkable title of Advisor to the Archbishop of Canterbury on Anglican Communion Affairs! You can see why the press cut it down to 'envoy', can't you? I didn't call myself 'envoy' and neither did the Archbishop, but the press said, 'We couldn't possibly manage that great title, so we'll use the word "envoy".'

How did we get on? Robustly, robustly! We had the sort of relationship that allowed both of us to joke together, to laugh together – and at times to be irritated and annoyed by each other; to be angry and say, 'Well, look here . . . !' – even though he was the Archbishop of Canterbury. We had a very open and good relationship.

And, I am rather pleased to say, that relationship is still maintained. We keep in very close touch. In fact, just before you arrived for this interview, he was on the phone saying, 'Do you think we might make a trip together again sometime, just for old times' sake?'

And I think we will. I think we'll be off again very shortly.

*Terry was instrumental in releasing three British hostages from Tehran in 1981, as well as four Libyan detainees in 1985. Later that same year, Terry made his first visit to meet the Lebanese kidnappers.*

Regarding the hostages, one had to make a deliberate choice as to whether to go public in the work, or whether to do it quietly. Now the reason for deciding to go public was that we wanted to make it known to the kidnappers that the Church was interested in being involved in setting up a dialogue. And that actually worked.

A letter came to Lambeth Palace as a result of my going public, signed by four American hostages, asking for the Archbishop of Canterbury to intervene. The kidnappers would never have allowed that letter to come out, had they not wanted to talk to someone independent, [and had they not realised through our going public that the Church was willing to talk with them]. That letter was as good as getting a visa to go and meet the kidnappers.

The point about this is, if you decide to go public and take a high profile, you can't suddenly turn it off. I've seen some curious accusations made. For instance, the wife of an American hostage said, 'When I went to see Terry Waite, he suggested that we might have our photograph taken together, and I didn't want that.' I remember that occasion, and I respected the lady's opinion, but nobody ever asked the question, 'Well, why did he want that?' They jumped to the easy conclusion that I just wanted my face in the paper.

Not so! What I knew was that there was a better chance, if the wife of the hostage had her face in the paper with myself, that that would get back to her husband in captivity. And it would have given him hope. He would have been able to say, 'Ah, something is being done.' One was conscious, all the time, of trying to send messages back to the hostages. I am as vain as the next man, but these attempts were misunderstood.

I know, from my own experience later in captivity, how much a message from outside can mean. That little postcard sent by a lady called Joy Brodier, showing the Bunyan window in that little chapel in Bedford, was the only communication I got from the outside world in those four years of solitary. Never despise the simple small action like this. You never know what hope or comfort it might bring.

It has been reported that the Archbishop of Canterbury said, 'Don't go,' and that I defied him. That wasn't true. He was, naturally, cautious. Admittedly, he wasn't 100 per cent saying, 'Right, yes, you go back.' What he said was, 'Well, you'll have to do what you think to be right.' He didn't stand in my way.

But looking back – and this is not reflecting on the Archbishop – you'll not find anyone who'll come forward now and say, 'Oh, we suggested Terry went back.' Not that I expected it: I took the responsibility. I knew the risks, and I did it gladly – and I have no regrets about that.

So I took up the invitation of the kidnappers to meet them. They told me that Terry Anderson and Tom Sutherland, both Americans, were very depressed and very ill. One of the kidnappers said, 'As a member of the Church, we will allow you to visit them.'

My response was the response that any ordinary normal person would make: 'You will keep me.' That is exactly what I said.

He said, 'No.'

I said, 'Will you give me your word on your faith?'

And he stretched out his hand, and gave me his word on his faith. It was very late at night when I was meeting this chap: it was about half past eleven at night.

I said, 'I can't come now, you must give me time to think.' Obviously one knew the terrific risks. I went away – he let me go away. I went back to think, and to take advice.

And the advice was what I expected: that if a word has

been given in that way it ought to be kept, but that – of course – there were no guarantees. You never have guarantees in those situations. And it seemed to me that it was one of those points in life where you have to say, 'Well, I've really got to go, because if they are telling me the truth – and there is the slightest chance they might be – and I walk away, what does that say about my own belief?'

Well, it is all mixed up. There is no such thing as a pure motive, not with me anyway. There was an element of pride in it: if I did walk away, I would have had to live with my conscience for the rest of my life. So there was a bit of selfishness in it, one has to admit that.

But I have said, time and time again, that the real battles are fought on moral and spiritual ground; I have said that one needs to have faith; I have said that we ought to try to do something for each other. And when the test comes to me, is all I can do to walk away, saying, 'No, I can't take that risk'?

So I went back.

*In January 1987, Terry was kidnapped.*

The actual kidnapping happened step by step. There have been ridiculous stories printed about my wearing a locator device. A locator device is, apparently – I have never seen one – something that is implanted on your person somewhere, either on your clothing or in your body, so that you can be tracked when you go on these dangerous assignments.

Well, people who write that stuff have never been to meet kidnappers! Because the first thing that happens there is that you are given a complete change of clothing. Then your teeth are examined, to see if anything is hidden beneath the fillings. Every scar on the body is probed and I can tell you now that if I had been wearing a locator device, that would be it – bang! Finish. One would be dead.

There there's a delay while you are moved to one house, where you wait a couple of days – the kidnappers are waiting to see if you are being followed – and then you are moved to another house. One expects all that. And the days went by.

But I had expected to be away for about a week or ten days at the most and, as more days went by, I thought, 'This is looking pretty bad.' Finally, I found myself pushed into a tiled cell underground. It was tiled completely. I remembered what Terry Anderson had said about the Lebanese Gulag – frightening! I knew, then, that this was it.

I said three things to myself at that point – out of bravado, really: I was afraid, so I said these things to bolster my failing courage. I said: 'No regrets, because I have done what I felt I had to do. No self-pity, because self-pity destroys. And no over-sentimentality.' By that I meant I wouldn't allow myself the luxury of thinking about family and friends in a way that makes one over-sentimental – looking back and saying, 'Oh, if only I had been a better father! If only I had spent more time with the children, if only I had done this or that . . .' That is being over-sentimental. You can't re-live life. So I made those three resolutions, and I did my best to stick to them.

I also decided to fast. I now think – I wasn't totally sure at the time – that it was principally for two reasons. One, it was out of anger and defiance. It was a way of saying to my captors, 'You've tied me up, chained me up, blindfolded me, put me underground, locked me in this miserable little box, and you leave me with nothing to fight back except my will. I am going to have some control over something, and therefore I will control as far as I can my eating. You will not get me to eat.'

So it was an act of defiance. It was also – and this is the nobler motive, because there are always a couple of motives (at least!) behind everything one does – it was also a way of saying, 'I must prepare myself for what's to come.'

I expected to face a rough interrogation, and I didn't know whether I would survive the experience. And fasting, when I had done it in the past, had had a remarkably strengthening effect on me. It gives you a clearness of head, a clearness of vision – and a strength of purpose that is invigorating. One of my favourite hymns is *Forty Days and Forty Nights*, and that's about the experience of Christ when, at a critical point in His ministry, He went away to be alone, to be by Himself, to fast and to pray and to gain strength for a great trial.

*At the end of a year in solitary, Terry had a gun put to his head.*

It came at the end of a very long period of interrogation, when I was very tired; emotionally as well as physically, very, very tired.

A party of men came into the room. Of course I was blindfolded, I didn't see them [I just heard them come in]. They said, 'You have five hours to live. If you have got anything else to tell us, you will tell us, and then you'll die.' And then they went away.

At that point, I lay down. I said the briefest of prayers. I felt terrific misery for a moment – largely for my family and friends, because I thought, 'They will never know how I survived up to this point, and how I lived these last days. And that's terrible for them.' That's how I felt.

And then I was so exhausted, I fell asleep. I actually slept for what must have been five hours – because I woke up as the men were coming back in the room. They said, 'Have you anything to say?'

I said, 'Nothing.' Because I had nothing to tell them; there was nothing I could tell them. And then I said, 'I'd like to write some letters.'

They said, 'You can write one.'

So I wrote a strange composite letter: to the Archbishop of Canterbury, to my wife, my children, my mother, some friends . . . I put the Archbishop first because I thought, if I do, there's a chance that the letter might get out, and therefore the note will get to my family and to the rest of the people mentioned.

I simply said in it what I still hold to. I told them that I was well, that I was in good heart – and I said, 'Try not to think too hardly about those who ended my life, because they have suffered much themselves.'

I gave the men the letter, and then they said, 'Do you want anything to drink? Wine, whisky, beer?'

I said, 'I'll have a cup of tea.'

We English! It sounds very funny now, I know. I don't even normally drink tea, I drink coffee. But tea seemed an appropriate drink then, I don't know why. I just felt like a cup of tea, so I asked for a cup of tea. And I got it.

Then they said, 'Stand up. Face the wall.'

I did, and I felt the gun at my head. I fully expected to die. I asked to say a prayer, which I said out loud: I recited the Lord's Prayer. And then I said a silent prayer: I prayed for my family and friends and colleagues. And privately I said the old, very familiar prayer, 'Into Thy hands, O Lord, I commend my spirit.'

And that was it. In some ways, you see, despite the natural fear, apprehension, pain and misery, I also felt, there is another side to it. Perhaps, in a short time, I thought, I'll have the beginning of the answers to the questions that have puzzled me all my life: what lies beyond the grave, what is it like? In a sense, there was almost an anticipation; almost a saying, 'This is an exciting adventure . . . ' Though that, I have to confess, was coupled with real feelings of fear, of misery and anxiety for others, and anxiety for myself also, because one wonders what it will be like to have a bullet through the head.

But, anyway . . . the gun was put down. I felt it drawn away.

One of the men said, 'Another time.' And he went away, and that was it. No more interrogation. The end of it.

Just four more years in captivity.

*Of the four years that followed, Terry spent three*
*alone. The final year of his captivity he spent*
*with Terry Anderson, Tom Sutherland and John*
*McCarthy.*

I was solitary for a total of four years, give or take a few
days. And during that time alone, my faith certainly didn't
stay rock solid.

I asked for a Bible, and I didn't get one for a long time.
And when I did get one, it was a new translation, and
I was disappointed with that. Not because I don't think
new translations are valuable, they are. But I hate being
so starved of beauty, of harmony, of music, of colour, of
rhythm, of companionship. What I needed was the beauty
of language, to breathe some harmony and beauty into my
hungry soul.

I can give you an example. In speaking of the prodigal
son, the old version of the Bible uses that wonderful
phrase, 'and he fain would fill his belly with the husks
that the swine did eat'. It has a wonderful ring to it. But
the modern translation just reads, 'and he had his dinner
with the pigs'!

The second thing is, when I read the Old Testament,
I read of battles and of people slaughtering each other,
knocking the daylights out of each other. At the very same
time, that was just what was happening outside the room
in which I was kept. Just down the road was the land we
call the Holy Land. Jerusalem. Just a few miles away.

Then I realised that the Bible, more than anything else,
gives us the truth about human nature very, very clearly;
straight between the eyes, no messing. And the truth that
one sees in the Bible is necessary. But truth by itself can be
brutal, and it can destroy; it can actually destroy people.
And in the situation of constant isolation and constant
examination, there is probably a limit as to how much
truth you can take.

When you come to the New Testament, you realise

that truth needs to be balanced with compassion. Where truth and compassion walk hand in hand, then there is a possibility of people growing up into their fullness as human beings.

But sometimes I was a bit irritated by the New Testament too, because people in prison there said their prayers and – *zap!* – they were out. And there was I, saying my prayers, and nothing was happening! One realises there is a whole world of difference between faith and superstition; between faith and magic. Christianity isn't magic. It is not a question of magic: it is much more profound and realistic than that.

In that confined space, in the situation of solitary confinement, one wasn't conscious of the warm, comforting presence of God. One felt sometimes very, very alone, and the voice of God seemed silent. One would have wished for almost, a voice to be whispering in one's ear, saying, 'Come on, it's all right.' There was nothing like that.

But one learned that God speaks powerfully in silence. That's a strange thing to say, I suppose, but it's true. It's somehow having the very deep assurance that, at the centre of the universe and at the centre of one's being, there is that powerful creative force that we call God, which is wholesome and creative; and somehow one is in communion with that.

And when one gets to that understanding, it opens up a whole new world. Church divisions seem footling. Even divisions between the major faiths seem to be footling: you can find a link point somewhere, find something that holds the human race together that goes beyond petty divisions.

I am now more, not less, tolerant of other people's faith, because of the experience I have been through. Temperamentally I don't like fundamentalism, no matter where it springs from: I don't have much fellow-feeling for Christian fundamentalism, or Islamic fundamentalism, or political fundamentalism. It has something so absolute in its expression! And because it is so absolute, it seems to me to deny the reality of the human situation.

I think it is most unfortunate for Islam that the whole of Islam has become judged by the action of a few extremists, who are by no means representative of the depth and breadth and beauty of Islam. *By no means* are they representative of that! And yet somehow, nowadays, there is almost a total, blanket criticism of Islam as a faith.

The time will come in the future when I might, just might, be able to make a contribution here. I'd like to have a small role in helping the dialogue between Christianity and Islam to develop and improve. I hope I might be given a chance to do that – because it is vital, I think, that the relationship is established at a deeper level than it exists at the moment.

*As soon as Terry landed at RAF Lynham, he made a speech that was broadcast live to a waiting nation.*

I felt, when I came out and made that speech, that it was doing two things. One, it was almost an act of defiance, it was saying, 'You have not beaten me: I come out even stronger in what I believe.' And it was also saying to myself what I really do believe, though it is very difficult to put into practice: that the real battles of the world are fought in the moral and spiritual realm. Politics are important but the real arena of battle is in the moral and spiritual realm.

It's not easy to say that, because you can be accused of being so pious, such a Holy Joe. And I don't mean it like that. I don't claim in any way to be totally morally upright and perfect – of course I'm not! But on that matter with the hostages, I tried my best to match my actions to my words.

I always used to say to myself, if I ever had the audacity to get into a pulpit and preach, I must remember when I speak that I may be called to get down from that pulpit and actually put into practice what I've been saying. I haven't always managed it – but on that occasion with the hostages, I tried to do it. And it was a bit costly.

I don't remember weeping when I came out, apart

from being very moved when I met the family for the first time: going into Lynham and seeing how Mark, my son, the youngest of our family, had changed. He was just a boy of fifteen when I was captured, and now here he was, a young man of nearly twenty-one. I didn't know him – I wouldn't have recognised him in the street. That was an emotional moment.

After so much solitude, it was difficult picking up relationships – not just with the family but with anybody. I found that I couldn't bear the emotional strain of sitting down for a meal with people for the first ten or twelve days. I used to sit down for a few moments, exchange a few words, and then go off to be by myself – and have a meal at two o'clock in the morning when it was quiet; when I didn't have to face the cut and thrust of emotional encounter.

But we received very skilled advice: 'Take it step by step. You've got time, you don't have to rush. Take it gently.' Good advice.

In the first weeks of captivity, I'd had a dream which I couldn't make head nor tail of: I was walking along a beach and I could see the sea coming in, and suddenly I felt terribly alone. And then I looked up and I saw a figure coming towards me and eventually I recognised this figure, and then two or three others, as my children. They took me by the hand and led me off the beach to the safety of a small town.

When I woke up, I thought, 'Good heavens! What does that mean?' It really was very vivid. Many years later, when I met Frances and my children for the first time since my captivity, my youngest daughter Gillian said, 'Daddy, take all the help that's going to be offered, do you hear?' They were – all of them – so really compassionate, even though they had been through goodness knows what! They were so supportive. And then I remembered the dream. 'Your family will lead you out.' How true that was.

But I don't think our style of family life has changed dramatically. I didn't say, 'Now I am going to spend all my time with the children because I've been away a lot.' That is not our family. We don't have to be in each other's pockets. I used to think that you always have to be together, do everything together – you know, that old idea of 'family, family'. That can kill.

It's a question of finding the balance: knowing that you can depend on family, that you are strong together, but that you can also have the freedom to be yourself, to do what you have to do as an individual. We can give each other space, and know – because we have passed through fire – that, when there is fire, we are, collectively, unshakeable.

And my relationship with Frances has been enhanced: my respect for her has deepened enormously. When I was captured, she said, 'My first responsibility is to make sure that the children have an opportunity to live a normal life.' And so she took the courageous decision to cut herself off from all publicity to protect the family, and I have enormous respect for what she did.

*Terry was shocked and hurt to be confronted with suspicion and criticism from the media – and even from some members of the Church.*

There was an attempt to say, 'Waite really knew about the arms, he was really involved in it.' There is nothing I can do about this. I wasn't involved, I didn't know about the arms. I know what I did and why I did it, and the reasons for going back.

I found it almost impossible to deal with the criticisms initially. They hurt, yes, and still do – because one has one's pride and one's sensitivities. It is easy for armchair critics who won't take risks themselves to know better, by hindsight, what one should do. The Church is a very human organisation. When things are running well, when the hostages are coming home from Iran or Libya, they all jump on the cart and throw their hats in the air. But when it's really tough, you find they have jumped off! You have to be prepared to stand alone.

One has to realise that, in the rough and tumble of the world, one moment you'll be hailed as the greatest thing since sliced bread and the next day you'll be knocked down. I remember clearly what my wife said to me, 'Never ever believe your media image, whether it is high or it is low. Believe what those who know you intimately tell you – you'll get a much better view.' I think she's right.

Oliver North asked to see me when I first came out. I wasn't up to it, physically or psychologically. Later he asked to see me again, and I said, 'On one condition, that the whole of our meeting is recorded.' He agreed to that. I wanted everything on tape because there was nothing I wanted hidden.

I am still a bit puzzled: how far was he the author of the plans that he put into practice? I think he was a man under orders. Let me put it this way, no Lieutenant-Colonel in the American military could carry off such an enormous plan without other people being very significantly involved. Who those other people were, I've no proof; I don't know.

What I felt about Oliver North in that role, he knows. I told him I disagree with that sort of political dealing, even though I recognise it happens all the time. On a personal level, I felt some degree of remorse in him about what happened to me. It was clear he had never, ever, expected me to return.

I don't think of myself as a hero. That's certainly not a definition I've ever given to myself – nor would I. I don't think there was anything at all heroic about what I've done. It depends, of course, what you mean by heroic. The real heroes, to my mind, are those we never hear about: the people who battle, day in and day out, with incurable illness or those who dedicate themselves to caring for the elderly, or those who work in hospices. These are the real heroes.

And there is Christ's supreme example of heroism. He refused to toe the politic line but stood by His humane calling – even though that led to His crucifixion.

I am full of powerful emotions. If you have got a powerful positive emotion, you are going to have a powerful negative one too, so I am a little afraid of my emotions. I recognise that within most individuals there is a tremendous power to create and destroy. I must learn not to be so afraid, but instead to be aware.

The charge that has sometimes been made publicly against me is that I can be a little too full of myself, too self-centred, self-important. There is a fairness in this criticism, I have to say. Other people can always see your faults so much more quickly than you can.

And I definitely ought to sharpen my capacity to really understand and sympathise, *empathise* with the feelings of others a little more deeply than I do. No, not a little more deeply, a lot more deeply than I do. That's a notorious failing, I think; a terrible one. And . . . oh, there are lots of failings. It's just a miserable litany when you look at it, really!

There is also another factor in my case. Often people who are physically out of the ordinary – very tall people, for example, and I am 6' 7" – can never escape being noticed. You stand out in a crowd and can easily develop a certain self-consciousness, a shyness. There is a shyness and a reserve, believe it or not, about myself.

I hope I have changed a little, from how I was before my capture. Probably I have made a small step – a very small step – along the road to becoming a little more constructively reflective. That I am pleased about. It is something I've wanted for a long time. To be a little more able to relax, to be confident that what I am doing is valid for me. In other words that it is perfectly valid for me to sit and to be quiet, and not to do anything other than to sit and to think and to pray and to read.

Now, although I've always said that that's something we all ought to do, in the past I felt a little guilty, because of my background. So I was always getting up and rushing around. Perhaps there's a better balance now, and I am glad to find that. It wouldn't bother me if I didn't have to travel overseas again. I like it when I do it, but I don't chase after it. I'm much more content to be surrounded by my books and papers.

I was enormously fortunate when I came out of captivity to be elected a Fellow Commoner at Trinity Hall,

Cambridge. They offered me a wonderful suite of rooms there, but I didn't want that. I wanted a simple room, not unlike a cell, in which I could recall my experiences. I used to go up there on a Monday and spend all day alone writing. On Monday, Tuesday, Wednesday, Thursday, I'd write all through the day.

The evenings in Cambridge I'd spend with my companions in the college. Marvellous people. We became really good friends, and that helped bring me back to life: the debate was good, the cut and thrust of argument. They didn't let you get away with a thing. I really wanted that: I needed to be stimulated back into intellectual life.

On Thursdays I'd go back home and be with the family. Some people have said, 'How extraordinary! After years away, you go and spend *more* time away.' But it was really essential to come back into things gradually, to find the balance between family, community, and being solitary. And as for being solitary, I find it necessary to have longish periods of time alone, three or four days at a time.

*On being a captive: the pain – and the learning.*

The physical brutality wasn't easy. It's scaring. I can't bear the thought of human beings actually being so callous as to deliberately try to mutilate the body of another. I mean, we have enough to face in this life without actually, deliberately, going ahead to mutilate and maim somebody.

And having no fixed sentence; never knowing when the term of imprisonment will end. That is a bit difficult. But then, in one sense, we all do it, because we never know when the end is going to come; when we are going to die. Someone said to me not long ago, 'The experience of captivity must be rather like the experience that faces those who have been told that they have a terminal illness. You never quite know whether you are going to make the end of the day, or the week, or the month.'

The way to survive, really, is the way in which we all need to live life – and that is, to live it in the moment. That doesn't mean to say you don't make sensible provision for the future, of course it doesn't. But it does mean to say that life is to be savoured *now*.

Sometimes I thought, if I ever get out of this place, what would I really like to do? Three things came to mind. First, I wanted to have time to read more, principally to read history and the classics, which I have always enjoyed. Second, I wanted time to write, which I hadn't had much time for in life, and occasionally to lecture. Third, I wanted to have time to engage *my* choice rather than somebody else's choice, in what I broadly term 'humanitarian activities'. And this I have actually done. *It is so important to live life*.

The other thing I remember now, so vividly, is coming out and feeling, for the first time in five years, the wind on my face. I thought, how lovely! Or seeing the colour of a flower, which I hadn't seen for years. How magnificent! These small things which, in the busy world in which we all live, we pass by. We don't see the exquisite colour of a flower, or say how fresh and wonderful that wind is.

That is living now; not living next week when, you say, 'I will be away on my holidays, and then I can enjoy this.' Or living for retirement. Living now. That's the way one really survived in those years.

What is true valour? Ah, I wish I knew the answer! I think probably it's having the courage and ability to face yourself as you are, to really look in, and make a frank acknowledgment of your own true condition. And to have the ability and courage to grow up as constructively as possible both for yourself and for others.

What all this is, of course, is a journey. It is a journey of exploration that one is making – that we are all making, throughout our lives. And the hymn that is perhaps closest to me is *Lead, Kindly Light*. It reminds me that truth measured with compassion is healing: otherwise it is a divisive sword. And it is also an expression of pilgrimage. I choose it because I think, for me, life is one constant pilgrimage, a constant search.

Having travelled all my life to pretty well every part of

the world, and seen many different situations and many different types of people, I think now that that's been interesting and informative, and I am very glad I did it. But I am convinced that the more difficult journey is the inner journey.

The journey of inner exploration is just as full of pitfalls as any outer journey. But it is probably more important, because it is a journey towards one's centre, to one's true sense of self and identity. And I believe that one can only find it in relationship to God. He helps us find our true identity.

I've likened it in some of my writing to a journey of exploration across the sea. The sea represents that great expanse within each individual, the expanse of the unconscious. And to set sail across those waters and to make that inner journey is both fearsome and wonderful – an exhilarating challenge.

One never ever ceases to learn from making that journey. Faith and Christian doctrine and belief – or, going beyond that, religious doctrine and belief – give certain tools, certain pointers for navigation. But at the end of the day, the individual, according to his or her capacity, stands alone at the point of death.

At that point, you go those last paces by yourself, across the sea. And, hopefully, into the hands of God.


## Lead, Kindly Light

Lead, kindly Light, amid the encircling gloom,
Lead Thou me on;
The night is dark, and I am far from home;
Lead Thou me on.
Keep Thou my feet; I do not ask to see
The distant scene; one step enough for me.

I was not ever thus, nor prayed that Thou
Shouldst lead me on;
I loved to choose and see my path; but now

Lead Thou me on.
I loved the garish day, and, spite of fears,
Pride ruled my will: remember not past years.

So long Thy power has blest me, sure it still
Will lead me on
O'er moor and fen, o'er crag and torrent, till
The night is gone;
And with the morn those angels faces smile
Which I have loved long since, and lost awhile.

*J. H. Newman (1801–90)*

# SUSAN HOWATCH

*I met novelist Susan Howatch at her flat in West-minster. She wants as little clutter in her life as possible, she says, so that she can be undistracted from her real work – to write what God wants her to write. So she has furnished the flat with a controlled and assertive plainness, which seems to reflect only one side of her personal mixture of certainty and shyness.*

*We talked in the main room, the one she keeps for interviews. It has a brilliant green carpet and four black, wrought-iron, upright chairs upholstered in bright green chintz, placed neatly around a laminated table. Apart from this, there were only two small sidetables and a bookcase, all apparently from the same matching wrought-iron set.*

*No curtains to soften the metal-frame windows. And no family pictures, no personal touches, not even books – all these must be kept in other, suitably private, parts of the flat.*

My family didn't go to church, except for the rites of passage – like christenings, weddings and funerals. But they definitely approved of the Church. They liked to know it was there, going on.

I very well remember my grandmother saying, in a tone of great horror, 'The new vicar has incense in the church!' And everyone said, 'Ooohh, how dreadful!' As if it were a great social *faux pas*. They were interested and positive about the church – so long as they didn't have to go there. My religious education came from school, which had a sort of Christian ethos but nothing too marked.

My father died when I was four. Though he went overseas when I was two, so I actually have no memory of him. I lived with my mother and grandmother for a time and then, after the war, my mother and I moved to a little house on our own.

I was a solitary child. I enjoyed my own company always, and I soon started to write. I remember learning the alphabet, and my grandmother teaching me. I thought, 'Oh, how exciting this is!' the first time I read my name: S – U – S – A – N. I can remember the great thrill of achievement.

I wrote my first short story collection when I was six – and I am bound to say that it was my last, because I never really took to the short story. I first started to write novels seriously when I was twelve, though I never spoke of it. It was very private and special.

These childhood stories can't have been any good. I've destroyed them all now, of course. I wouldn't want anyone to read them if I fell under a bus tomorrow. They're all gone with the wind. But it was all training, and the more you write the better you get at it, you hope.

I remember the Coronation in 1953. I was thirteen, and it was my first experience of a big religious service, and it was very powerful. It was powerful pageantry and, particularly, a powerful religious service, in Westminster Abbey – the local shrine, around the corner from where I live. It's now my local church.

I would say I was a Protestant of the Middle Way of the Church of England. But of course it is very difficult to pin labels on. I'm what the Archbishop of York would call a Conservative Liberal. I believe in the importance of tradition, but I believe in the freedom to interpret it for today. Also, I approach things through the intellect: I tend to be distrustful of great emotional binges.

One is quite wary of the emotions. In the eighteenth century there were people who had a great suspicion of what was then called 'enthusiasm'. I think I'm rather like that. I guess it's a typical stiff-upper-lip British syndrome, really. But hymns very much remind me of great moments of my life. When I listen to some of these well-known hymns, I can feel all the emotions welling up, because that touches something inside me.

But I think when you get into deep emotions in crowds, it can be very ambiguous, very ambivalent. One thinks, 'Is it from God, or is it from the Devil?' That is, of course, old-fashioned picture language. You really need to be very careful because a lot of it is induced from the unconscious, and that can be very unhealthy.

I don't play an instrument, but I do enjoy listening to music, especially in church. I don't actually have a CD or a record player, or whatever they're called nowadays, because I like silence to live with. But I do enjoy hearing music in church.

I started being interested in classical music in about my mid-teens. When I was twenty-one some cousins I was very fond of gave me what we used to call in those days an LP, a long-playing record of extracts from Handel's *Messiah*. And there was one track that I particularly liked, which I played over and over again, and that was *Comfort Ye, My People*.

I think when I got this record, I was quite disturbed and troubled in many ways, because life in England wasn't working out for me too well. I think, on a subliminal level, music promised comfort for the future. And I thought, maybe it'll all be all right in the end. 'All shall be well, and all shall be well, and all manner of thing shall be well,' as Julian of Norwich said.

*After a law degree, a year as a trainee solicitor, and a short spell as a secretary, Susan decided to move to New York in 1964.*

Nothing was really working out for me in England. I'd just had a manuscript turned down. I'd been submitting manuscripts for seven years and had been rejected many times every year. But finally I had one manuscript that I thought was particularly promising, and I was even encouraged by Collins, the publishers, to re-write it. But then, in the end, they still turned it down. And that was really too much. So I thought, 'I must get out of this country.'

Also I had no boyfriend, and of course when you are a young woman you really do need to have a boyfriend: not just for one's own personal satisfaction but also as a status symbol. Certainly in those days one did.

I thought, 'Oh, I'm a failure in my personal life, I'm a failure in my professional life – I must get out from under. Just nothing is going to gel in England.' So I went to America with an old school friend of mine. And immediately I set foot on American soil, everything went right! I had my social life, I met my husband, and I got a book accepted for publication. It was as radical as that.

I wrote *Penmarric* while I was over there because I was homesick. Even though America was very good to me, I still, naturally, hankered for England. My English friend used to hanker for Walls' pork sausages. One did have one's yearnings for England. When I was writing *Penmarric*, I could see Cornwall so very clearly, because I was longing for it. It was a place I had visited when I was much younger, many times.

*Penmarric*'s success surprised me: it was like a dream story. During my twenties I had written six little mystery books – about one a year – and sold them directly to paperback publishers for fifteen hundred bucks a throw. All very minor stuff. They had a shelf life of just six months. But all the time I was working on *Penmarric*, my labour of love.

I hoped it would get published, but I wasn't very certain. Then finally I took it to an agent, and she said, 'No, it's too long, go away and cut it by a third.' And I did, and when I went back to her, nine months later, she said, 'Well, I never thought I'd see you again.'

But she sold it over a weekend, and then – it was really amazing – it took off and sold all over the world. That put me on the road to success.

I was only thirty or thirty-one, and suddenly I had money as well as fame. Yes, we are talking megabucks! I still did live quite simply for a time. We didn't move house, though we paid off the mortgage in one whack

– but then, gradually, it got more and more glamorous; though I never went in for things like mink coats. I'm not a minky person. I did have a Mercedes and a Porsche – but not together! And I had a studio apartment which faced the Manhattan skyline.

I remember my husband and I went out to dinner one night. We had champagne, and the waitress said, 'Oh, what's the special occasion?' And my husband said, 'Oh, it's just another Tuesday night.' That's the sort of mindless, rather amusing thing that one quickly gets tired of. But it was fun at the time.

Success, actually, is very difficult to handle. I think that it had a profound effect on my marriage, although there were other things going on there too. It was very difficult. My marriage broke up in 1975, about four years after *Penmarric* was published. I decided to leave America with my daughter, and we went to live in the Republic of Ireland for four years. When I was there, I wrote four other very long novels, the successors to *Penmarric*.

I preferred to be quite secluded then, in order to write. But I wasn't able to be really alone, because I had my daughter with me – and because people in Ireland were so friendly. And, in those days, the 1970s, I was still on a roll. I was more jet-setting than ever. I remember once I went from Dublin to New York for dinner, and I jetted each way on Concorde: that was the sort of lifestyle. I did try and damp it down a bit. But the real changes in my life didn't happen until after I left Ireland and returned to England.

*After her return, Susan went through a profound change of attitude towards her life.*

I remember very well the first Christmas I was back, in 1980. I tuned in to the Nine Lessons and Carols from King's College, Cambridge, and I heard that wonderful treble solo of *Once in Royal David's City* – and suddenly I could just see myself back in kindergarten. I thought, 'Yes, now I'm really reconnecting with my roots, and perhaps I'm going on to a new life.'

I still wasn't religious but it was definitely bringing me in touch with my school days, plugging me into that vaguely religious ethos at school that had permeated my early life.

There's a verse in it which I particularly like – although maybe it's mere Victorian sentimentality:

> And our eyes at last shall see Him
> Through His own redeeming love.

That, to me, goes to the heart of the Christian faith, to the concept of redemption: the fact that, even though we make mistakes and make hashes of things, we can be forgiven and we can be redeemed and go on to a new life.

I had thought that once I was back in England I'd be free to live happily ever after. In fact it was the reverse. I became increasingly dislocated: I couldn't settle anywhere. I tried to settle in Cambridge and couldn't, I tried London . . . and I realised, very dimly, that I was looking for something.

One day I saw an advertisement for some flats on sale at Salisbury. I'd only been to Salisbury once, but it had struck me as being a very peaceful, serene place. So I thought, 'Well, I'll go and get one of those.' I ran down to Salisbury, and bought a couple of flats, little ones: one to work in, one to live in.

But when I moved there, I felt even more alienated. I was having problems with my publishers over the final long novel I did. And then my daughter decided to go to America to live with my husband. That was sad – and of course one always has guilt about all kinds of things. Show me the man that feels no guilt and I'll show you a psychopath!

I think the best thing is to face up to guilt and admit it. I think far too many people repress guilt and then it erupts in other, more disruptive ways, and makes the person unhappy again. It's a Christian theme, this: if you sin, you have to repent, and if you repent, then you have the chance to be forgiven – or to forgive yourself, which is important – and to go on and redeem the situation, to make it good. Then you have a resurrected life.

My daughter came back to England after a couple of years. Now she lives quite near me in London; that rift was all patched up, that's all okay at the moment. But during the early 1980s, I felt – just as I had in the early 1960s – that I was coming up against a brick wall in every single direction: personal life, professional life.

I felt completely alienated. I couldn't really speak to people. Luckily, in Salisbury everyone was so well-mannered and polite, they only said 'Good morning' anyway, so I didn't have to say more than 'Good morning'. But silence is very important, that's what I've found. In fact, you find God in silence. I think the problem today is that there's too much noise: people have a radio dribbling all the time, or the television on. You can't hear properly.

Throughout this difficult time, Salisbury Cathedral was staring me in the face. But I didn't make any connection with it because I wasn't a churchgoer. Once, though, after dark I remember very well passing by the window of my study and looking out – and there was this wonderful, floodlit animal outside: the cathedral at night. And then I did gasp.

It was during this time in Salisbury that I had my 'enlightenment', as it were: I did my 180 degree turn. I'm sorry to say it wasn't a 'Road to Damascus' experience, with flashing lights – what fun that would have been! I should have enjoyed that. No, it was more mysterious and alienating. And it had been coming on for some time before I was really aware of it.

Gradually I realised that, by serving myself all these years by struggling to be rich and famous and successful, I'd made myself very, very miserable; so perhaps the time had come when I had to serve something else. And when I started to fish around for what else I could serve, then I began to grapple with the whole concept of God.

It seemed to be very evident that there was something out there closing in, and something in here welling up. It was not my conscience exactly. My conscience was in an absolute fog. I didn't know what was going on! As I said, I was very disorientated. But I thought, 'Well, why not give the premise that there is a God a whirl. Why not give it a try?'

It seemed a good, intellectually sound position to take at this stage of my life. Why didn't I assume that there was a God, that this thing closing in on me and shaking me until my teeth rattled, was actually God – and then see where that got me to? I thought to myself, 'Well, I've served myself and made myself miserable. Maybe I should start to serve God.' So the next question was, 'Well, okay, what does God want?'

Functioning as I do through the intellect, I thought, 'I'll do some research: I'll start reading.' And once I started reading, I was hooked. I fell in love with reading theology, and I thought, 'Gosh, why don't more people know about theology?' It's riveting – all about the real issues, like, 'Why am I here? What's it all about? What should I do next?'

Then I thought, 'Maybe I'm supposed to teach theology: go back to college, get another degree, and teach. Maybe I'm not meant to write at all.' I decided just to keep on and see where I got to. I did an A-level course in religious studies, and the deeper I got into the subject, the more fascinated and intrigued I became.

There was no longer any question but that God was there. And that it was up to me to find out what He wanted and do it, in order to become a more whole, a more integrated, version of myself.

I started writing again in the shadow of the spire of Salisbury – even though I wasn't at all sure at first whether I was supposed to go on writing. It took some time before I was quite sure I was meant to do that. In fact, I read for about eighteen months before I actually picked up a pen and began to write the first of the Starbridge novels.

When the manuscript was finally finished – and I did seven drafts because I found it was so difficult, it was so different from anything I'd done before – I put it away in a drawer. I thought, 'Well, maybe I'm not supposed to publish it.'

But then I found I *had* to write the next Starbridge book! When my agent came over from America, I showed both her and my British agent the books, and they said, 'Yes!' and were very excited. So I thought, 'Okay, I am meant to publish, I'm not meant to teach: I'm meant to go on writing, but in a very, very different way.'

I said to my agents, 'The second novel is about two monks talking for the first 150 pages. Can you imagine anything quite so uncommercial?' They took it quite well. I think they were nervous, but they were very supportive. I just thought, 'Well, if God wants me to do this, I must do it, and not worry about what happens.'

But the books did incredibly well. The sales go into millions. One's only human and so one does like to be successful – and of course writers do like to get feedback from people who have enjoyed their books – but what I feel very strongly is that, in a sense, it's not my job to worry about all that any more. My job is simply to write the books as well as I possibly can. When I finish the book, I offer it to God and I let it go. After that, it's up to God. If He wants me to be on the bestseller list, then that's all right, but it's nothing to do with me any more. In the old days I would have agonised about it and thought, 'Oh, goodness me, am I going to be at number three this week or at number five?' Now I think, 'Even if only a couple of people read the books, so long as they help maybe one person, that'll be fine by me.'

I wasn't sure at first how many books there were going to be in this series, but halfway through the second book I knew there were going to be six. Now I think I've finished. I've had some requests to go on but, artistically speaking, it is a whole.

I wrote in this series about spiritual journeys, on Christian themes of sin, forgiveness, redemption, repentance,

resurrection and renewal. My clergymen got into awful
jams: sometimes sexual ones, or they drank too much.
They went off the rails in various ways, but they repent
and strive to do better.

But the characters always come first, otherwise they
don't become real. The Christian action grows out of
the characters. If you think of the theme first, and then
hang the characters on it, the characters won't resonate
properly. But if you're doing the creation right, and I
hope I have, the theme should actually grow out of the
characters and the kind of people they are.

My characters sin only because they are very unhappy,
not lined up right with God. And they come to integration
by finding out what has gone wrong.

In the 1970s, I was marketed as a romantic novelist.
But as I have always been so interested in the psychology
of my characters and how they relate to reality, the last
thing I wrote – even in the old days – were romances. I've
never really been interested in romance: I'm interested in
reality.

*Susan came across Jungian psychology through the
writings of the Christian theologian Bryant.*

I write, obviously, to satisfy my neurotic needs. You'll
never get a writer admitting that to you, but of course
that's why we write! We're all neurotic in a way, aren't
we? Certainly I'm neurotic, but I hope I've managed to
adjust to it so that I can lead a more integrated life. I
think the first thing one has to do is to face up to one's
neuroses. That's like facing up to one's guilt, isn't it?
And you've got to pursue the truth all the time. It's not
so easy.

I think there is a route to God through self-knowledge.
Medieval mystics certainly believed that your first task
is to know yourself. The Christian faith believes in two
aspects of God: there's the transcendent God who's up
there and out of this world, and there is the immanent
God, who is buried like a spark in the soul of each human

being. And to get to that spark, to line up your ego with your true self, where God dwells as a spark, is actually a spiritual task.

What I am really talking about, in modern language, is 'integration'. How to be a well-integrated person. God created each one of us for a purpose. What one has to do is find out who one is, so that one can be – or become – that person that God wants us to be. And that is the spiritual quest, the spiritual journey, that we are all called to undertake.

One of the high points of my conversion experience had been when I came across an entry in the *Dictionary of Christian Spirituality* for 'the second journey'. It described in detail what I had been going through. I was so relieved to see this entry, because I had thought I was going mad.

A 'second journey' is when you come to the end of one phase in your life and you go through a period of great darkness, where all the milestones, all the markers shift. And then it all clarifies and gels, and you go off again.

When you get to those crossroads, you either go sideways and try something quite new, or you go on, on the same path but in a completely different way. As I have said, when I got to my own personal crossroads, I wondered whether to go sideways and teach theology, or whether to go on writing, though writing very different kind of books – which is what I did. That was my second journey. My first journey was behind me, and I didn't want to cling to it.

I think there should be much more knowledge circulated about this business of the second journey. I think it happens to quite a lot of people, though not necessarily everyone. For some people, the first journey may be all they require to become the people that God wishes them to be. I believe you can have three journeys – or even more. I believe Beethoven had three: the *Quartets* were his third journey.

Then of course you get the people who don't realise their potential, who don't become what God requires them to be. I think if more was known about this phase, then it would certainly put a lot of people's minds at rest. It put my mind at rest, knowing that I was going through a certain syndrome. I didn't have to be frightened any more.

*After four years of living quietly in Salisbury, Susan decided to move to London – and settled into her modest flat in Westminster.*

I realised I couldn't live without a big church in my life, so I thought, 'Oh, a flat near Westminster Abbey – yes, that's what I want.'

From then I did begin to go to church regularly. I try to go most days, although I don't always succeed. I like evensong very much – matins is a bit boring, I think. And the eucharist I find very difficult. I don't take communion yet. I think, actually, that whenever two or three believers get together and sit at a meal and break bread, that should be Holy Communion. I'm just objecting to the fact that it's become very rarified and stylised, and doesn't seem, to me, to have much to do with Jesus.

However, having said that, I respect the fact that this is the way that the majority of Christians can tune in to Jesus, and tune in to God. My way is to be absolutely alone, in silence before a cross. That's how I can focus best on God and Jesus. This is a weakness. I'm not bragging about it. I'm working on getting better at worship. In another five years I hope I will say, 'Yes, I'm a communicant, I've finally got over my hangup.'

I try not to have too many things in my flat. It's important not to have too much clutter. Otherwise you spend all your time tending to the clutter, and you don't have enough time to really figure out what God requires, what you are supposed to do next. I did try and pare myself down. I haven't succeeded as far as I'd like. I think it is an on-going pursuit, because one accumulates clutter so quickly.

A lot of emotion goes into my work, a lot of energy – a lot of sexual energy. I'm very much in favour of sex. I believe it is a very powerful force, and that all human beings have to make up their minds what to do about it: whether to be heterosexual, homosexual or bisexual. So it's something we all have to think about, and be honest about. But I think sexual energy is something that can be used in other ways: you don't have to just copulate madly every night! At this particular time in my life, I choose to channel this energy into my work. Whether this will continue to be so in future I don't know, but it was certainly the only way I could have lived for the last ten years.

I think you have to harness emotion carefully, otherwise you can just waste it all. It can waste you. But I hope I'm not so drained of emotion that I can't have my circle of friends or relate properly to my family. I am sometimes frivolous and let myself go – you check with my friends! I think God probably has a sense of humour; one would imagine so. Jesus would certainly seem to have had a sense of humour. After all, He had a good time at the wedding feast, didn't He, changing the water into wine? I wish somebody would come along and do that for me!

I wish I was fundamentally more gregarious. I find it quite difficult to do what the theologians call *kenosis*, and pour myself out, as it were, towards other people. When I'm working, I pour my whole self into my books – but I wish I was better at giving more of my time and myself to other people, which is another aspect of Christianity, of course.

If I were more relaxed about emotion, I think perhaps I could relate to worship better. I find worship very difficult; I'm very stupid about worship. That's the handicap of approaching things through the intellect. As it is, it just seems very peculiar. Maybe, not being brought up in a religious home, it just seems very strange, like a sort of esoteric activity performed by people on another planet.

The vicar of the Close in Salisbury said to me once, 'Susan, worship has to be worked at.' I found that rather helpful. It's rather like the spiritual equivalent of jogging. It's good for you. If you don't go to church, the danger is that either you become narcissistic or you might go over the top and go rather peculiar.

I think a lot of people today think worship is a form of entertainment, and it's not: it's something that has to be worked at. In the kind of Anglican worship I go to, you are an individual within the group. It's not all people joining hands and singing and clapping, it's not that kind of thing.

*In 1993 Susan gave £1 million for the creation of a lectureship in Theology and Natural Science at the University of Cambridge.*

It is quite tricky to part with £1 million – I mean, a million is a million, isn't it? But it was definitely something I was called to do.

It seemed to me a very good idea if people came out of the different disciplines and started talking to each other. Some people seem to think that theology has something to fear from science. I would say the best religion has nothing to fear from science, because it all takes place in God's world. It all comes from God and it's all part of the unity of knowledge. I think, in the twenty-first century, scientists and theologians should all talk to each other.

I think Beauty, Truth and Goodness are absolute values. That's an old-fashioned concept, but I happen to believe it's true. I don't believe in the grand doctrine of relativism, post-modernism: I think that would set our whole culture going down the drain. No, I believe that there are definitely some things that are better than others, and that not all views have the same worth and value. I believe myself that Christianity has very great value. I believe it's better than, say, some sort of cult that worships a tree. We do have to make choices; there are values.

And although I don't think clergy should run for Parliament, I think that they should definitely speak out on the issues of our time, because Christianity is a way of life. People seem to think it's a way of death: that you only turn to Christianity if someone's dying. In fact, someone asked me the other day, 'Was there a death in your family that led to your conversion?'

I'm going to be ashes and dust eventually. We all are, aren't we? People don't like to think of that. That they'll be ashes and dust. But we are talking about Christianity and Eternal Truths: how to live your life, how to get the best out of your life, how to be well-integrated; we're talking about Jesus Christ, who said, 'I am come to give them life, that they live it more abundantly.'

I have a crucifix in my study, hanging over my writing table. It's not a crucifix of Jesus just hanging, looking miserable. It's a stylised one of Jesus looking triumphant, a *christos victor*. He's got His hands stretched out, and it's a very hopeful, positive, dynamic sort of image. Before I start work in the morning, I always look at it for a long time, just to psych myself up.

But very often one's aware of God at less obvious times – perhaps if one's talking to someone who's suffering, or perhaps someone who's homeless, selling their magazine. It can happen at any time: I might be shopping in Sainsbury's. Ours is a religion of the incarnation, so we can meet Jesus anywhere.

## Once in Royal David's City

Once in royal David's city,
Stood a lowly cattle shed,
Where a mother laid her baby,
In a manger for His bed,
Mary was that mother mild,
Jesus Christ her little child.

He came down to earth from heaven,
Who is God and Lord of all;
And His shelter was a stable,
And His cradle was a stall:
With the poor and mean and lowly
Lived on earth our Saviour holy.

And through all His wondrous childhood
He would honour and obey,
Love, and watch the lowly mother,
In whose gentle arms He lay:
Christian children all should be,
Kind, obedient, good as He.

For He is our childhood's pattern:
Day by day like us He grew;
He was little, weak, and helpless,
Tears and smiles like us He knew;
And He feels for all our sadness,
And He shares in all our gladness.

And our eyes at last shall see Him,
Through His own redeeming love;
For that child, so dear and gentle,
Is our Lord in heaven above;
And He leads His children on
To the place where He is gone.

Not in that poor lowly stable,
With the oxen standing by,
We shall see Him, but in heaven,
Set at God's right hand on high;
There His children gather round,
Bright like stars, with glory crowned.

*Cecil Frances Alexander (1823–95)*

# MARTI CAINE

*I met comedienne Marti Caine at her house in Oxfordshire, which has floor-to-ceiling plate-glass windows and a panoramic view over open fields that takes your breath away. Inside, the house is equally striking in its openness: pale uncluttered floors glow against white walls, and all the furnishings are plain and white. Even the cups in her kitchen cupboard are white, and all their handles point at exactly the same angle.*

*For Marti is obsessional about cleanliness and order – and she does all her housework herself. She even sewed the white curtains and upholstered the white sofa. Did she really? Actually, Marti confides, no, she didn't: Lynne did it all. And who is Lynne? Why, Lynne is her other self.*

*Once I've stopped reeling and taken in this idea, she continues cheerfully that she has two quite distinct personalities – at least. There's her colourful and outrageous stage persona, Marti, and then there's Lynne, her 'real self', who is quiet and loves being at home.*

Marti is completely different to me. She gets me into terrible trouble, she says outrageous things. I think, 'Ooooh, who said that?' – and it was me, as Marti. Marti Caine is impossible to live with and Lynne Ives is boring, but between the two of them – hopefully – we get something like a reasonable human being.

When I'm driving up the motorway, I'll be observing the rules, sticking to the speed limit – and suddenly, the chin juts out, and I realise it's her behind the wheel. She's infinitely more aggressive than me. *Aarrrrr!* the car goes, and I think, 'Omigod, she's taken over again!'

She's very strong, I have to keep her down. I don't have her anywhere in the house at all. There are no photos, nothing to do with Marti Caine whatsoever, anywhere in the house. All her clothes are in the loft and any pictures are in the office, locked away.

I chose the name Marti Caine because I wanted something androgynous, like 'Dusty Springfield' or 'Kiki Dee'. I didn't want to be 'Julie Rose', or something like that. I was Sonny Smith for a week, and I was Zoe Bond for a week – and then I thought, this is no good at all. So Malc, my husband, reached for a book – it was a gardening book, as it happened – and we'd choose a page at random, say page 57. So he'd turn to page 57. Fourth line down. Third word along . . . 'Greenfly!' No, try again. Right, page 92. Fifth word down. Now, what is it? 'Tomato cane.'

'Oh,' he said, 'That'll do. Call yourself "Marta Cane".' So I rang the club and said, 'Hello, Zoe Bond won't be able to come tonight, it'll be Marta Cane.' And he said, 'Right.' And when I got there, I found he'd mis-heard and put 'Marti Caine'. In coloured chalk, mind you, which means you are something – you're a ten quid act if you get coloured chalk! So I was Marti Caine from thenceforth.

*Marti was born in Sheffield in 1945.*

I had marvellous parents, very loving, very gentle. Especially my dad. My mum was a bit fiery, though she was very beautiful. My dad died when I was seven, but I remember his gentleness.

My first memory of hymns was *All People that on Earth do Dwell*, because my dad and I used to clean our teeth to that every morning. '*Alllll peeeople that on eeeearth doooo . . .*' by the time you'd finished the song, the teeth were clean. And I used to think it meant: '*All people that on earth who have do'ed well*' can '*sing to the Lord with mighty voice*'.

When my father died, the thought that I'd never see him again was devastating. I think that's when I really started believing in God, because I needed God to assure me that

I'd see my dad again. After a few weeks, the wound healed over, on the surface at least. But his death changed my mother completely. She started to die the day he died.

She couldn't cope without him at all. She couldn't sleep, so she got some sleeping tablets from the doctor's and then discovered that if she took them during the day as well, it reduced her to a state of semi-awareness, and so she started taking more and more and more. And within a very short period of time was hooked on them. Then she discovered that if she mixed them with alcohol, which she never usually touched, it made them more effective. It was a gradual process. But eventually she had become hooked on alcohol as well as sleeping tablets.

Still, kids are very resilient. I just stepped in and took over, without even thinking about it. I was perfectly capable. I did it because I had to, I suppose.

*At the age of nine, Marti was put into care in a children's home.*

I was only there for six weeks at the most. Newspapers and magazines have made such a lot of this. It sounds very Dickensian when you read it, but it was pleasant enough, considering. But I did run away.

I got a penny, a platform ticket, and got into the guard's van – on the opposite platform to where I had got off the train, so I presumed it would take me to Sheffield. But it didn't, it took me to Carlisle, where I was discovered by the guards. They plied me with Penguin biscuits, and saucers full of sweet tea and so I gave them my grandfather's name and address and place of work, and he came to collect me.

My grandfather figured largely in my childhood. He didn't have any religion at all. He thought that when you live, you live, and when you die, you die, and that's an end to it. Your children provided eternity for you.

When I was little, I adored him, I thought he was absolutely wonderful. He would come home from work, have his tea and come straight round to visit me. He always took me to bed and read me a story, every night. He spent all his time with me, he taught me to read – and when my father insisted that I wore Kilty Start-Right lace-up shoes and had them measured, my grandad bought me bright red sandals, which we'd hide in the garden hut and I'd wear when I was with him. He used to do all sorts of sneaky things that my parents wouldn't have approved of – which of course won him the hugest place of affection in my heart.

He was a pattern maker, so he made me some wonderful toys, very professional: a blackboard, a doll's house, a shop, musical boxes, a desk with a roll-top and leather tooling and a stool to match. He converted the garden hut into a Wendy house, because Princess Anne had just got one. It had two little chairs and a little drop-leaf table in walnut, a three-armed light fitting, a television with a picture of the Queen stuck on to the screen and knobs that actually clicked.

Once he made me a wooden scooter with wheels, painted bright red and blue and yellow. I was going down the road on it, delighted with my new scooter, when I hit the kerb, and went over the handlebars. So he picked it up and smashed it. You'd have thought he was trying to kill a poisonous snake, the venom and hate he put behind this scooter, because it had had the temerity to tip me off. He was strange.

From the time I was eleven, I was living permanently with my grandfather. But he was very domineering; he was a very strong, tyrannical man. He had so dominated my father's life that my mother said to me, 'Whatever you do, don't let him make you do what you don't want to do, because otherwise he'll crush you.' But I was the apple of his eye so I could do anything with him.

After a while, my friends stopped coming. They wouldn't stay for the weekend. They tried to tell me why, but I didn't understand what they were saying. They would say, 'Well, I am not coming this weekend because your Pop comes into our bedroom.' And I thought, 'So what? He is probably just checking to see if we're all right.'

And then it happened to me and I finally realised why they didn't come any more. What he did to me was virtually nothing at all, but it affected me for the rest of my life; even now it affects me, even though my experience was relatively minor. So for those who are totally abused sexually, I have the greatest sympathy, because I know what far-reaching effects it has.

I felt betrayed. I felt unloved. I felt I had loved a stranger, someone I suddenly didn't know. He wasn't my Pop any more. And I felt jealous as well, because I realised that he had been giving attention to my friends, and that made me very jealous. It was a strange mixture of feelings.

My life was saved, or my spirit or my soul was saved, by a very good man – a teacher called William Lowe. He was a very religious man. In fact, he is in his late seventies now and running a Christian shelter in Australia. Goodness shone from his face. He loved all of us and we all loved him, and I wanted to 'dood well' for Mr Lowe. I think he was the person who made the most profound impact on my life.

I was thirteen at the time I came under his influence. I'd been ruling the roost from the age of seven and was very wilful. I had been going to the Locarno to all-night dances from the age of twelve, looking more like a twenty-six year old. I'd been to fifteen or sixteen different schools by then. Whichever school I was at, I presumed I'd be moving on soon, so I never bothered. I used to spend most of my school days in the girls' toilets waiting for home time, knowing the teachers wouldn't miss me since they didn't even know I'd arrived at their school.

But Mr Lowe spotted me. He cherished me and nurtured me. He brought me up to date with my maths, with my history and geography – and actually read out my very first essay. It was the first time anybody had read an essay of mine out. And he congratulated me in front of this classful of strange kids. Phew! I felt like a super star.

From then on I wanted to do everything right for Mr Lowe. I stayed in every night instead of going to the Locarno, looking up my history, looking up my geography, practising my maths, writing essay after essay after essay. I used to find a list of big words out of the dictionary and find a way of weaving them into my essay, just to please Mr Lowe. Sometimes I think that's where I belong, with a pencil in my hand, writing; I think that's maybe what I should have done.

Mr Lowe's secret was that he loved us. He loved all of us. It was a genuine love, and that's all it was: there was no ulterior motive.

*When she was sixteen, Marti became pregnant. She
married Malcolm Stringer when they were both
barely seventeen; by the time they were nineteen,
they had two sons, Lee and Alex.*

I'm not very mumsy. And of course the older I get, the more I lash myself with guilt – but that goes with the territory of being a mother, doesn't it? Anything that goes wrong with them, if they get a boil or whatever, it must be because I smoked, or because I didn't give them enough liver.

I feel terribly guilty about the things I've said. I never hit my kids, I could never hit them; probably because I feared that, if I did hit them, I'd not be able to stop. Sometimes – you know what kids are like – they drive you barmy, don't they? They can really drive you to the end. So I never actually hit them, but I said some terrible things. I probably did more damage with my tongue than I could ever have done with my hand.

Being a mother isn't easy. I know it wasn't easy for my mother either. When I was twenty-one, my mother killed herself. She took an overdose, one of many. But this time it worked. There's nothing I could have done to stop it, I don't think. She was so soft and sweet, but it was her state of mind, or her state of spirit.

I didn't feel guilty. I had said all the things I needed to say. I had told my mother I loved her, and she wrote a letter to me before she did it. My mother killed herself,

I didn't kill my mother; she did it herself because she didn't want to live any more. She'd been pumped out so often that it was like having an open wound, that you keep shoving your finger in. Eventually it grows callouses around the outside and you don't feel the pain as much, you become de-sensitised. I'd become de-sensitised because of her very many attempts at suicide.

And by that time, anyway, I'd realised that we're all responsible for our own lives. I'd realised the truth of the old adage: 'If it is to be, it is up to me.'

I did all sorts of part time jobs while the kids were young, to make ends meet. I worked delivering flowers to pubs, I worked in a chip shop, cleaning offices, as a waitress, I worked in a cutlery factory, sharpening knives . . .

*. . . And doing spots in working men's clubs. Constantly having to cope with new surroundings during her childhood had taught Marti a useful skill.*

I had got my first laugh at the age of seven – all the kids falling about, and pats on the back, and 'Come to our party', just with one laugh! I couldn't believe the power of it. I was invited to all the parties because I was the class clown.

There's not a big leap from being the class clown to being a comedienne at working men's clubs. It's the same beasts you are working with: you've still got a hostile audience, be they seven-year-old kids or a working men's club audience. You are still trying to make yourself popular to strangers, trying to make yourself accepted. That's all it is really.

*But Marti's big break came when she won the grand final of* New Faces, *a television talent contest, in 1975.*

My agent said, 'Look, they are doing auditions for *New Faces*.' But I didn't want to do it. I was a star, for goodness sake, I didn't do noons!

In case you don't know about 'noons' and 'neets', in the working men's clubs, you did two spots on Sunday afternoons (the noons), and then you went back on Sunday evening and did three night spots (the neets) – unless you were a star, in which case you didn't do noons, you only did neets.

I said, I didn't audition, good heavens! People knew what my fee was. If they wanted me I was eight quid a night. My husband was only earning fourteen quid a week, so eight quid a night was a considerable amount of money.

All I wanted was a fitted carpet and a three piece suite, that's why I was doing the clubs. Just to provide. I always wanted a nice home. One that I could look after myself, which is why I would never be happy in a palatial mansion. I wouldn't like cleaning staff: I want to clean my own windows and do my own washing and my own ironing. I like it, it keeps me self-sufficient.

Anyway, I eventually did do *New Faces*. And the grand final that year had some very good names in it: Lenny Henry, Victoria Wood. Aye, I won – and shot to the middle, while they have soared to the top!

Of course I don't think of myself as a star – if I'm a star, what's Frank Sinatra? I'm here temporarily, I'm aware how fragile it all is. I'm amazed that it's lasted this long; I imagined it might be three years.

I look upon success as being fated; not so much heaven-sent as a challenge from heaven. It's very easy to become puffed up with your own self-importance, especially when you've got an adoring public. It's so easy to lose sight of the fact that you are very, very, very fortunate to be earning all that money purely and simply because you can't type. That's why most of us are in the business, let's be honest, it's because we can't do anything else!

And I certainly wouldn't want any more fame, I certainly wouldn't want America or the rest of the world. Losing your anonymity is a bit like losing your virginity: you'll never, ever get it back again. It's great for a fortnight, but after that it turns you into a prisoner.

And the more fame you get, the more of a prisoner you become. Ask Elvis Presley, ask the Beatles. Even in my small way, I'm only really happy when I'm here within these four walls, because here is where I can be me, Lynne. If somebody comes to the door, or the phone rings, Marti Caine answers. She comes out, so I'm invaded, my privacy is interrupted by another person – in the shape of Marti Caine.

*Despite marrying so young, and being a teenage mother with constant financial difficulties, Marti's first marriage lasted eighteen years. They divorced in 1980.*

He fell in love with someone else, it's as simple as that. I don't think he intended to. I don't think either of them intended to. It just happened. Your head can't always rule your heart.

I certainly loved him far too much to stand in his way and say, 'You're not leaving.' The kids were grown up, one was seventeen, one was nearly sixteen. I did beg him not to go, but he was in love and there was nothing that could be done about it. At least he was honest, he didn't deceive me. I think deception is a bigger killer than infidelity. And because we could talk, there was a lot of understanding. Malc is still one of my best friends.

I always bear in mind that it says in the Lord's Prayer: 'Forgive us our trespasses as we forgive those who trespass against us.' In other words, if I forgive others, God will forgive me: if I don't, then He won't. And He's got an awful lot to forgive me for, I'm afraid.

In fact, it would be quicker to tell you what my not-faults are than to list my faults. I'm not envious – and that's about it. That's the only deadly sin I don't possess. I've got all the others: I'm bolshie, I'm aggressive, I'm terribly difficult to live with. I'm a perfectionist. You should see my cupboards! All the cup handles point the same way – which is why I'm so difficult to live with, I suppose.

I hope God has got a sense of humour. Oh dear, yes,

please God, have a sense of humour! And I think He understands and forgives. You read about these people who do horrendous things to kids, and you think they have got to burn in hell; but then I don't think God would be happy with the thought of any of His lambs in Hell. I think He's got to forgive us all.

But I also think everybody pays, one way or another, for their ill deeds. It might not be something that's apparent to the rest of us, but we all pay one way or another. Before we get up there, our debts are cancelled out.

I think God has got to have a fantastic sense of humour. It's got to be fun, religion. Religion is so heavy if you're not careful. It's a drudgery, if you only go to church because you're going to be struck with lightning if you don't. We shouldn't be like that. You should go to church – or temple, or synagogue, or whatever place of worship you go to – because you want to. That's why I love gospel music. I think gospel singing is fantastic. It's such great fun and everybody enjoys themselves and gets everything out of their system. Steam comes out of their ears!

*In 1985, Marti married Kenneth Ives, a BBC producer. Three years later, she had to face a crisis, when she was diagnosed as having cancer.*

Well, it was certainly a new challenge. Not a challenge that I'd ever had to face before – I'd enjoyed trouble-free motoring all my life, so I can't really complain. And I never ever felt that I was dying. I just didn't really believe it; I felt perfectly healthy.

In fact, I had far too much energy. I've always been very energetic, and this particular time I'd got so much energy that I put on ankle and wrist weights, and a body thing that I made covered in curtain weights, and I used to run round the fields here to try and get rid of the excess energy.

But I looked thin. Malcolm, my ex-husband, knows me inside out and upside down; he knows if I've lost even a pound. Because when I'm depressed, I ring him up and say:

'Oh, I'm thin, I'm thin!'

And he says, 'You're not thin, you're just depressed. Get on the scale, you'll weigh eight stone four.'

So I go and get on the scales, and come back and say, 'Yeah, I'm eight stone four.'

And he says, 'See, I told you, you are just depressed.'

But this time even Malcolm said. 'My God, have you lost weight? You look horrendous!'

Though I felt great. The day I was hosting the final *New Faces*, I was wearing a black sheath dress, a silk jersey one. An hour before the show these two lumps came up in my groin about the size of golf balls, and they showed through the dress. It looked very weird, and I had to change my outfit.

About four hours after the show, the lumps went down. I felt all right, so I didn't think any more about it, but a few months later I had to go for my annual check-up for insurance purposes and they discovered a strange blood condition. It's something to do with the amount of time it takes for the sediment in your blood to settle.

The doctor said, 'I don't know what it is, because you are A1 in every other direction; it must just be a virus that you had, that you didn't notice.' And I thought, 'Well, I wouldn't mind having it again because I've certainly had a lot of energy these last three weeks.' I was just due to go on holiday, so the doctor said, 'Go on holiday, and when you come back, we'll have another blood test and it'll probably be all right again.'

So I went on holiday, and whilst I was on holiday I got three lumps under my arm. I went back to the doctor's, and he said, 'I think we'll do a biopsy, but I think it'll be all right, don't worry about it.'

They did a biopsy – and it turned out to be not all right, much to my surprise and everyone else's as well. Five years was the average prognosis for this particular type of lymphoma; there are about two hundred odd different types. Some are easy, some aren't so easy. This one was considered terminal. 'Treatable but not curable' is what they said.

It sounds stupid, but I wasn't frightened – because I didn't think I was going to die. It was such a cushy cancer. Had I been in pain, it would have been completely different, but I had no pain, I had no symptoms whatsoever. I had no tiredness, which is the usual symptom, no skin complaints – I had nothing, nothing at all. If the doctor hadn't told me I'd got cancer I wouldn't have known. In fact, I wouldn't have known for the last five years. The worst part of it has been the treatment, and even that wasn't as bad as I thought it would be.

But Kenneth's reaction was panic. And my family: panic. Not obvious, outward panic but their eyes screamed. They surrounded me. I was knocked out: I couldn't believe how much my friends cared for me. They were there, like a shot. And the response from the public was overwhelming. Thousands upon thousands upon thousands of letters, all supportive, all saying the right things, all caring, giving me advice. Phenomenal. If you could bottle that stuff they gave to me, you could give it to everyone else and save them. I am sure it saved me.

I don't think I could have got through my illness without a belief that (a) if you die you are going to a better place, and that (b) with help from a Divine Being or an Omnipotent Presence, you can survive. If you haven't got sufficient confidence in yourself, I don't think you can do it alone. *Breathe on Me, Breath of God* said everything I needed to say to God during the last six years.

I believe in God, firmly. It's not a belief, it's a certain knowledge – I've heard Him. All right, some people call it 'conscience'. But I've always been aware of God. I know the concept of Jesus Christ is difficult to accept. But there are other concepts that are difficult to accept and we know them to be facts. If you consider that every snowflake, every blade of grass, every leaf, every living creature is entirely different to any other – is unique, completely unique, every single one of all the billions and billions of snowflakes that fall per second, every single one of them is unique – well, that is a fact. But it's an even more difficult concept to take on board than the fact that God impregnated a virgin and Jesus Christ was born.

I talk to God all the time – which is, I suppose, praying. I don't actually get on my hands and knees, close my eyes and put my hands together, because I think you can talk to God anywhere, any time. You don't need a church, and you don't need your hands together. You just need a desire to talk to Him, and the answer will become apparent.

If you ignore it, well, that's down to you, but the answer is always there. I think you always know the answer to your problem in your heart of hearts, it's just that you won't admit it – because it might not be what you want to do.

Being ill confirmed something that I already had a suspicion of: that everything happens for the best; that often the best things in your life are what you consider the worst things in your life. Like getting pregnant at sixteen: I thought my life was over. Getting cancer: I thought my life was over. In fact, it turns out that my kids are the joy of my life, the best thing that ever happened to me. And I have learned so much from this cancer, I've gained infinitely more than I've ever lost. All I've lost is four pounds, a bit of hair and my nails, and they have all come back again – except the four pounds, though I live in hope!

What the cancer has taught me is that you get more out of adversity than you ever do out of your good times. I've patched up old, imagined quarrels. I am less willing to compromise because I realise how short life is. Even if you live for a thousand years, it's still too short; you never actually have time to do all the things you wanted to do.

I also realise that when you realise your mortality, at the end of the day, it's the things you haven't done that you regret, not the things that you have done. And there are so many things that I haven't done yet, that I must do before my Maker collects me. Though even if I live to be 94, I doubt if I'm going to get them all in.

I've been told that forty per cent of people who have had bone marrow transplants for this particular type of lymphoma will not get a recurrence, but sixty per cent will. So by the law of averages, it will come back. But when it does, or if it does, I'm prepared for it. There are things that can be done; it's not the end of the line.

Apart from which I've had such a good time, one can't complain anyway. I've got two wonderful kids, a wonderful grandson, I've got some wonderful friends, a wonderful husband, a wonderful ex-husband . . . all I can see is goodness. I think if you look anywhere you'll find good. Hidden under the evil perhaps, but you'll find it given half a chance. People are wonderful; people will give.

What has kept me going has to do with medical science mostly. Positive thinking certainly helps, or at least it makes it more bearable. And a belief in God. I'm in His hands entirely. If He decides to come and take me, He'll take me when He's ready, and that's that.

But I'm not dying, I'm living! And I won't be dying until you hear me take my last breath: then I'll be dying. Until that day I'm living, and it's wonderful. Life is wonderful. Life is a celebration. It really is!

I think love is the answer to everything. That's all that's needed, really, and I was given so much from my parents. It must be awful to be a kid that doubts that his mother or father love him. I never, ever, had a single doubt that I was loved and cherished more than anything else or anyone else in the world by my parents and my grandparents. For the first seven years that I existed, that wrapped me in cotton wool and protected me against everything that was to come.

Love . . . Love is everywhere. Gardening is a form of love; it's loving the earth, loving nature. Mr Lowe loved us; he loved all of us. They say in Yorkshire that you can do more with a carrot than you can with a stick. I think that's true. Love! Love is the answer, God's love, your parents' love. Just love.

## Breathe on Me, Breath of God

Breathe on me, breath of God,
Fill me with life anew,
That I may love what Thou dost love,
And do what Thou wouldst do.

Breathe on me, breath of God,
Until my heart is pure,
Until with Thee I will one will,
To do and to endure.

Breathe on me, breath of God,
Till I am wholly Thine,
Until this earthly part of me
Glows with Thy fire divine.

Breathe on me, breath of God,
So shall I never die,
But live with Thee the perfect life
Of Thine eternity.

*Edwin Hatch (1835–89)*

# STEPHANIE COLE

*She had just been filming her latest sit-com success,* Waiting for God, *just down the road. And although Stephanie Cole had barely moved into her tiny cottage in Warwickshire when we met, she had already made it look like home. There is a huge fireplace that takes up almost the whole wall, and in nooks all over the cottage there are paintings, wooden carvings and intriguing books on psychology and on exploring a range of spiritual paths.*

*Stephanie hadn't yet had time to get going on the garden – but she loves having her fingers in the soil. So as it was a beautifully sunny day we snatched a few moments to see what could be done.*

*What was clear was that, even if Stephanie never did anything to her garden but simply left it wild, she would still have a spectacular view – of three lamb-filled, green and pleasant counties, Warwickshire, Oxfordshire and Gloucestershire, meeting a little way beyond her fence.*

Coming back to live here is, in a way, circling back to my roots – but roots I didn't really know about. I was born in Warwickshire, my mother was born in Warwickshire, and my father was born in Warwickshire, but we left it when I was very young. I even rediscovered my half-sister recently, living near by, after many years apart.

And it's beautiful countryside. So when I was looking for somewhere peaceful and serene, I thought, 'Let's have a look in Warwickshire.' It is certainly easier to remember one's faith in surroundings like this than in the hustle and bustle of the city. You can hear the still small voice much more easily when you're in peace and quiet, can't you?

This morning, I woke up (I don't have any curtains at my bedroom window, because I love being woken by the sun, and I love seeing moonlight) I woke up and it was a glorious day. I looked out at the hills of Gloucestershire, at Warwickshire and Oxfordshire, because I can see all three counties from my window. The beauty takes your breath away. And it is so easy to believe, it is so easy.

But then I have to go back to the city and test it, you know: test my belief. I have to say I wouldn't like to live here all the time, for the very simple reason that I think I might become a bit – dare I say it – complacent. It's too comfortable here. So I need to get out there and test it.

As a child, I moved from Warwickshire because we were bombed out. A German coming back from Coventry had a bomb he hadn't used, so he popped it down in our back garden. So we moved, to a tiny seaside village in north Devon. My childhood was spent swimming, searching the sands for shells, playing games with imaginary playmates in the sand dunes. It was idyllic.

Since we lived by the sea, the sea was very much part of my life. I learned to swim almost before I could walk. And I went to this tiny little school in a place called Braunton, and we used to go to church every Sunday. The hymn that always got me was *Eternal Father, Strong to Save*. When I heard 'for those in peril on the sea', I used to stand there crying. I'm not quite sure why: I didn't know any sailors – I certainly didn't know any drowned sailors. But it was tremendously powerful stuff.

When I was a kid, I never had that traditional idea of God as a man with a great white beard, up in the sky. God was always *a bend in the river*. Now I know that sounds slightly strange. But behind the sand dunes there was a little stream, with a little wooden bridge over it. My beloved great-aunt used to take me there on walks, and when I was old enough I used to go there on my own. It was a very special place for me: the river came from sunlight, curved into the dark under the bridge, and then curved out to light again.

This was when I was about five or six. And for some

reason, whenever I thought of God, this bend in the river was the picture I had in my mind.

When I was seven, my mother re-married and so we moved again, this time to south Gloucestershire. We were in the middle of the country this time, in a farming community. So my feet and my hands were once more in the soil. That closeness to the earth was part and parcel of my childhood, and has always been very important to me.

This time there was a river at the bottom of our garden. And again there was that wonderful bend in the river, where you went from light into dark and through to light again. So that's how it has always been: God is not the old man in the sky but this bend in the river.

But that simple, unconscious childhood faith didn't continue. It didn't just waver: in my late teens I completely lost all faith. I can remember when I was about seventeen or eighteen, someone said, 'Oh, he did very well, thank God.' And I got very angry and said, 'Don't thank God, thank him, the person, he was the one who did it!' So at this stage of my life, I completely rejected everything about God.

*Stephanie became a student at the Bristol Old Vic Theatre School in 1958.*

Acting is a way of discovering a bit more of myself. I have to go into those parts of myself that I might not otherwise have explored, in order to play those parts in a character. And what it leads to – at least, in my experience – it leads to a better understanding of other people. Because you have to keep stepping into other people's shoes.

It's like when you meet somebody for the first time and you think, 'Oh-oh, I'm not sure I like them very much.' And then you think, 'Hang on a minute, Steph, hang on a minute! Just step into their shoes for a second, walk in the other man's shoes and just see what it feels like, and then perhaps you'll understand why they are like that.'

Anyway, that's what I hope that people will do with me

– so that there's a certain tolerance and understanding towards this lunatic woman! Seriously, I do think stepping into someone's shoes can lead to more understanding.

People are often surprised to find that I am actually much younger than many of the parts I play. In fact, the very first time I earned money acting was playing a ninety year old! Nowadays I suppose I am best known as the grey-haired pensioner Diana, in *Waiting for God*.

We were recently filming in Brighton and I was in the full costume and makeup, with my grey wig on, when this woman came up to me and said, 'What are you doing here?'

So I said, 'We're filming a series called *Waiting for God*, for the BBC.'

'Oh, yes?' she said. '*Waiting for God* . . . Who's in that, then?'

'I said, 'Well, Graham Crowden and Stephanie Cole.'

'Oh yes, I know Stephanie Cole,' she said. 'She's George Cole's mother.'

Now, I'm a great admirer of George Cole but I am *not* his mother, nor am I old enough to be. I took that to heart: that was upsetting!

But actually most people say, 'You're much younger off the television,' which is very cheering. Though the day will come when I won't be – unless they then start wanting me to play women younger than I am. Oh, that's a lovely thought, isn't it? Maybe I shall end up Juliet, the only ninety-year-old Juliet in the business!

Another older woman I played was an army widow, the Alan Bennett character in *Soldiering On* from his *Talking Heads* series. She was a valiant woman, I think. Usually when you think of valour, you automatically think of people doing amazingly brave deeds. But today I think of valour as just putting one foot in front of another – particularly in the world in which we now live, it can be very hard, with the recession and so on.

There's also something very personal here. I have a brother who's schizophrenic. For me, anybody who manages to live every day with an illness like that, putting one foot in front of another, staying alive, is incredibly brave, incredibly courageous. I think true valour is keeping on keeping on.

I hate that idea of my being a 'charity lady' doing 'good works'. I do have three favourite charities. One is the National Schizophrenia Fellowship, because of my brother. I am deeply committed to that, and I do as much as I possibly can for them, because it's very much a Cinderella charity. People are very frightened of mental illness. One of my dearest wishes – though I guess it won't happen in my lifetime – is that one day the fear of mental illness will not exist. Even now, some people can't admit that they have someone in their family who is, say, schizophrenic. The fear makes it absolutely taboo. One of my ambitions is to help disperse that.

I also work for Age Concern – because I'm sort of an honorary pensioner I feel I have a great affinity with pensioners – and anyway, in a few years I'm going to be one. I also do a fair amount for CRUSAID, again for obvious reasons. Aids is a disease that has hit so many of my friends and colleagues in the acting profession. I will do as much as I can – but it is very selfish, you know: I do it because it makes me feel better that I'm actually doing something.

*Stephanie's marriage ended in 1988. She hasn't re-married.*

As far as sharing my life with somebody is concerned, of course you are more wary after you have had a difficult experience. You think, 'I don't want another failure like that; I don't want to hurt myself or somebody else like that again. I must surely learn from this where I went wrong, what I did wrong.'

When my marriage started to go wrong, I felt that it was very much my fault. So I took myself off into analysis, and it was through analysis that I actually re-acquainted myself with my spirituality. I rediscovered that part of me, the very spiritual part of me, that had not been fed in any way, shape or form. It had been ignored for years.

An extraordinary homesickness would well up in me – but for something that I didn't know. How can you feel homesickness when you don't know what you're being homesick for? But I did. And I started to ask myself: why? From where? What for? And these questions almost inevitably lead one into: what do I believe in? Why am I here? Why are we here?

I suppose, in a way, I had become a humanist, although I wouldn't have known what that meant in those days. But when I began to feel that gap in my life, I started – just out of interest – reading the occasional book about various belief systems. And that's really what started the journey back.

I studied other faiths, and I know it sounds so trite to say, 'I was a Buddhist for three years,' doesn't it? But Buddhism was the first of the other faiths I explored. Then I looked at Hinduism and read the *Bhagavadgita* and then I looked into all kinds of other religious traditions. It wasn't that I threw myself into any of them completely, I was just reading and searching.

I suppose I was trying to find things that called to me, and I did find things in all of the belief systems that I read about. But nothing *fitted*. Little bits meant things to me, but nothing actually fitted me.

Then I started reading the psychologist Carl Jung. When a patient went to him, one of the first things that Jung would say was, 'Go back and search in the faith in which you were brought up, because that will have echoes in your unconscious.'

And I thought, 'Hmm, well, Jung was right about an awful lot of things, so maybe I should go back and have a look at the faith in which I was brought up.' And that was how, by a circuitous route, I returned to my religious roots in Christianity. It was a very gradual process. There was no blinding light or anything like that.

Although there was one moment, I remember, that meant a great, great deal to me. Around the time I'd

started searching again through Christ's teachings, the
BBC re-ran the John Freeman interview with Jung.
Freeman was talking with this extraordinary man who
was now in his eighties, and there came a point when
Freeman said:

'Now you were brought up in a very strict faith, but after
everything that you've been through, do you still believe
in God?'

And there was this amazing moment when Jung said,
'No, no, I don't believe in God . . . ' – I held my breath
– 'I *know*.'

*Ahhh!* I literally leaped off the sofa. I was on my own,
and so I shouted, 'That's it!' That's what I want. That's
what I want to go towards, where I can really, honestly –
with the whole of my body, mind, soul, everything – can
say, 'I know.'

So that's what I'm going towards . . . But it seems to
me that you can't strive for it. It's something that will
happen.

*But the years of searching didn't strike Stephanie as
wasted.*

If anything, the going away made the coming back better
for me than if I'd just stayed put. It meant that I had
looked at all sorts of other horizons, other possibilities
and how many of those horizons were actually all part
and parcel of what I'd left. But now I could see them,
where previously I couldn't; I had been unconscious to
them, during the period of my simple, childhood faith.

The best way I can explain what happened is by
making an analogy with rehearsing a play. You come
to the first read-through, and when you read the script
your instinct will be spot on. And you then go through
that painful period in rehearsal where you're finding out
why your instincts were right! So from ignorance, through
knowledge, back to an innocence. And that's what for me
the journey has been about.

It was as if I was born with that inner connection; and

then I went through the dark and tried to find out all the whys and wherefores and all the head stuff; and now I'm coming back to what I came into the world with.

Analysis has given me the ability to choose. It's like undoing a piece of knitting – undoing this great mass of old, matted knitting which doesn't actually help you to enjoy life, to celebrate life, to *live* life. When something happens in my life now, I can knit it again either according to the old pattern – but consciously this time, knowing that that's what I'm doing, choosing it – or I can say, 'That pattern doesn't actually do anything to look after me. This time I'm going to choose a different pattern.'

So it has helped me immeasurably, to come to terms with who I am. To start to actually *like* who I am – and not to mind if other people don't. That's okay. It's all right!

Of course that doesn't mean despair and frustration have disappeared. They're here every day of my life, you know. Of course it's not all sweetness and light.

In the Gnostic Gospels, Jesus said, 'If you bring forth what is within you, what is within you will save you. If you do not bring forth what is within you, what is within you will destroy you.' But the bringing forth seems to me to be like that saying in the Gospels: 'Narrow is the gate and strait is the way.' It refers to that process of finding out about yourself and coming back to who you are – which is, for me, a part of God's way. It is a very, very painful way, a stony way. But I also believe that the things that you find along the way, and the ultimate experience – which comes after death – are well worth the sweat pouring off one and the cut feet.

There are various places that I go to for the kind of inspiration I need – for example, St James's, Piccadilly. It's a church that has eclectic ideas and invites all sorts of speakers; things happen there which are very exciting.

I also go up to Findhorn, which is a big spiritual community in Scotland. When I go for a walk and I get to the top of a hill – and then I see there's another hill which is a little bit higher and will give

me a better view, I always think, 'Hmm, I might have
to go to the top of that one next and have a look.' I have
to go. So when I'd heard all about Findhorn, I thought,
'Go on, then, Steph. Want to find out? Well, go, have
a look.'

It's a very large community. I think there are about
two hundred permanent members, and at least two or
three hundred people visiting – sometimes for a few
months, sometimes just for a week. I suppose it's a
sort of experiment in community living, with a tremendous spiritual bias. It's very eclectic, very broad based.
The bias is towards Christianity, but it encompasses
all belief systems. There is room for everybody there,
which I like.

I have been there many times over the years. It's a
place of enormous peace and quiet, with 'sanctuaries' –
places for meditation or prayer. I'm a loner – who also
needs people. I'm terribly gregarious: I love talking to
people, I love finding out about people, I'm endlessly
curious about people. But equally I need solitude. Just
as I need bread and water to live, I also need solitude.
For me, Findhorn has been a place to retreat to. But
now that I've got this cottage here, I might not need to
go any more.

*There is a large wooden cross on Stephanie's
window sill.*

That was made for me by a carver at Findhorn. Spiritual symbols like this seem to me to be tools: tools
that I can use in order to transcend. That's why I
asked the carver to make the wooden circle around
the cross. You can go *through* that circle to the other
side.

I think the danger is that sometimes people get stuck
on the symbol – for example, on the symbol of the cross.
It always seems to me that the suffering of Christ on the
cross is not so much an end in itself, as if that suffering is
the be-all and end-all; but it's through that suffering that

you get to the other side. We talked earlier about 'narrow is the gate and strait is the way'. That's about crucifying the ego, as it were, in order to transcend. So for me symbols are reminders of what it is that I'd like to *get on the other side of*.

There are one or two things about New Age-y places that I'm uncomfortable with, like the tendency in some people to see everything bathed in light while ignoring the dark. I don't think you can have one without the other – and I think there's a danger in ignoring the dark forces within us that we need to acknowledge.

But in any belief system there are going to be things that, because we're human beings, are a bit iffy and that doesn't mean you have to throw it all over. It's like a river, isn't it? A river flows along and comes to a big rock in the middle of it. Now what does the river try to do? Does it try and shift the rock? Does it try and bore through the rock? No, it just flows round it, or over it.

There was a lot to do with Christianity, too, that I used to find difficult. And I have to say that I still bump into things about it that I find difficult. But now I just think, 'Well, this part doesn't work for me, but that's okay. It doesn't mean that all those teachings are wrong, it just means I can't quite encompass this particular thing at the moment.'

I don't believe in original sin. Where did the idea of original sin come from? It certainly didn't come at the beginning of Christianity, did it? Actually, I have a great belief in 'original blessing'. There is, in fact, a tremendous movement in the Church now – in both the Catholic Church and the Protestant Church, I believe – that is called 'creation spirituality', and is to do with this idea of original blessing.

There's a wonderful Wordsworth poem, which seems to encompass the idea that we come with original blessing rather than original sin. It's from the Ode *Intimations of Immortality* and it goes:

Our birth is but a sleep and a forgetting:
The Soul that rises with us, our life's Star,
Hath had elsewhere its setting,
And cometh from afar:
Not in entire forgetfulness,
And not in utter nakedness,
But trailing clouds of glory do we come
From God, who is our home . . .

And that's what it seems to be about: that we come from this amazing source of light and energy, and we are part of that. I think that's why some people say, 'I'm God.' Of course if you say that, people will give you funny looks and say, 'Oy, oy . . . ' But we are all part of God, we are all a little bit of this amazing thing.

To explain what I mean, imagine being born. There you are and there's this hosepipe coming down straight from God to where you are. But during the course of your life that hosepipe gets all tangled up and knotted, and the water won't flow through: the energy from God will not flow through. And so you spend your life – I've spent *my* life – trying to untangle the hose. What happens then is, as it gets more and more untangled, it's easier for that energy to flow through and you become a channel really. Hopefully. So I suppose it's not too surprising that one of my favourite hymns is *Make Me a Channel of Your Peace*.

*Beyond the cycle of 'coming back to who you are' within one lifetime, Stephanie also describes a longer-term cycle of being.*

I have a great friend who is a very wise lady with a wonderful idea. She says, 'Think of all the people who are very important in your life, and make a list of them.' It can include the milkman – somebody who comes every day into your life – or it can be somebody who is dead, who was very dear to you, or whoever.

And then, against their name, in a second column, put the first quality that comes to your mind when you think of them: perhaps 'kindliness' or 'modesty', or 'directness' – or maybe even 'spitefulness'! So you put that in the next column. And in the third and last column, you put where you meet them: where they come into your life – at home, at the office or wherever.

Then you label the first column, 'My Teachers'; the second column, 'My Lessons'; and the third column, 'My Classroom'. I think that's a wonderful way of looking at life, rather joyous. So if good things happen, you can think, 'Well, that's great.'And if bad things happen, 'Well, what can I learn out of this?' I don't mean that that response will be the first thing that occurs to one, because the first thing is whatever emotion is evoked. But after that it's, 'Okay, so what actually have I learnt, what can I learn?'

My feeling is that the soul has to be refined and refined, until it can go back for ever to that place from which it comes, that source of energy. So you keep being born until you've got it right. You know there's a saying, 'You choose your parents'? I like the thought of my soul sitting up there and looking down, thinking, 'Okay, kid, so what's the lesson this lifetime?' and, 'Okay, that's a good parent to choose if you want to learn that particular lesson.' And down you go.

My personal belief system encompasses the idea of re-incarnation – but it is a very personal belief. I wouldn't *ever* try to change anybody's mind or influence them, because I don't think that's the purpose of our being here.

Do I go out and proselytise? I can think of nothing worse! That's total anathema. I loathe it when people try and thrust their ideas down my throat, and I would hate to think that I would ever try and impose my beliefs on anybody else. I think to impose *any*thing on someone else is incredibly arrogant! So *no*. I never even introduce the subject of my beliefs into a conversation. But very often the subject will come up, and then I will exchange ideas – but I wouldn't want to be in the least bit evangelical.

There's a huge difference between serenity and smugness. Smugness is, 'Well, I've got it right. I don't know about you, but I've got it right, and I'm all right.' Whereas serenity is, 'Listen, I don't know whether I've got it right, but if you really want to know what it seems like for me . . .'

Serenity seems also, for me anyway, a willingness to encompass change, to be flexible; it's not to be stuck. Smugness always seems to be frightfully stuck – you know, you're *smug*, sitting with your fat bottom in a comfortable armchair: whereas serenity is like floating, changing, moving amoeba-like . . .

*Stephanie shares her cottage in Warwickshire with her daughter.*

I have to disagree with people who say that acting is a cut-throat profession. It is ambitious of course, because we all have to live with our egos. But I think the great thing about being a human, not just an actress, is to run your ego and not let your ego run you. Rarely is that more obvious than in the acting profession, for obvious reasons.

But I think you'd be hard pressed to find another group of people who are so willing to work together, to trust each other, and offer huge support and love. I remember my daughter coming to us one day and saying, 'I've decided what I want to do, I want to come into the business.'

She wanted to work backstage. I was thrilled – and she said, 'Why are you so thrilled? Is it because I'm following in your footsteps?'

And I said, 'No, no, no, it's nothing to do with that. It's because this profession has given me such a good time that the thought that you're coming into it is great. Of course it has hard times, some piggy bits, but it's all right.'

*As a result of her appearance in the* Sweet Inspiration *television series, Stephanie has been asked to write her autobiography. So now she is looking back, more than ever, over her life and the values that have given it meaning.*

It seems to me that it is all to do with love, it's all to do with unconditional love. It's one of the hardest things to learn, and I can't even begin to say that I have learnt it. Maybe I've just touched it every now and again. But that seems to me what it's all about: learning unconditional love.

And that kind of love, of course, encompasses the whole: everything and everybody, every living thing. Not in any pi way, or sweetness-and-light way: that's really *yuech*, because it's ignoring the fact that everything and everybody has their dark side as well. We can't exist, can we, without that dark side?

And I can't exist on my own. What would I be without other people and other things? There'd just be no point! The point is interrelating with others and enjoying other people and feeling unconditional love.

I used to think, 'What on earth am I here for, what on earth am I doing?' Now I think 'Well, I don't know. And maybe I won't know till after I die – and even then maybe I won't know! It'll have to do, not knowing.'

It always seems to me that people are terribly afraid of not knowing – do you know what I mean? It's terribly secure, isn't it, when you know? 'Here is my house. And here is my garage. And here is my car. And here are my children.' And so on and on. 'We know this and we know that.'

But *not to know* is often very scary. Though I actually think that not to know can be immensely thrilling. I actually like not knowing. I have a favourite piece of music, *Adoramus Te, Domine*. It means, 'We adore Thee, Lord', and it's beautiful. Those are almost the only words: just 'Adoramus Te, Domine'. It just repeats and repeats and repeats those words – and actually I think one can transcend with that, just as one can transcend with a *mantra*. It takes you out of yourself, so that you can experience that great white bubble where your mind ceases to be that busy little ant, running from thing to thing and thought to thought, and just is at peace.

It's not swimming against the tide, it's floating on the water; just floating there, knowing that it will take you, you'll get there.

I'm frightened of dying, but I don't fear death. I have a fear of pain – one would be a fool not to be afraid of the pain that many people have to face – but I don't fear death itself. In the last two or three years, I've realised that thinking about death has become very much a part of my life. I've thought about it, I guess, every day. And it seems very important, as I grow older, for it to be part of my life.

Death also seems, to me, not to be the opposite of life. For me, it seems rather to be the opposite of birth: it's another transition that we go through. It feels to me, actually, as if it is another birth – a birth into something else. So no, I have no fear of death itself, not for myself nor for the people who are dear to me.

What's my idea of heaven? I'll tell you what it's like: when I think of that, or of death, it's like going home. *I can go home now.* That is what it feels like – although I don't know what home looks like. It's a feeling, more than a picture.

I know what I would like my epitaph to be. The North American Indians have a wonderful phrase to describe a successful human being – not successful in materialistic terms, but successful at actually living what they say they believe, instead of just rabbiting on about it – and I would love to get to a stage in my life where people could honestly use that phrase about me: 'She walked her talk.'

When I was a student, and then an aspiring young actor, the great catchphrase when you were acting was 'play the now'. It seems to me to be equally valid for life: play the now.

Obviously, the past informs the now, and what you do in the now informs the future. But it seems to me to be very important to be *in the moment.* Yes, I know that now is a chaotic time in the world, deeply chaotic and deeply frightening. I think it's terrifying for everybody, and that's why people go to such extremes: extremes of violence, extremes of religious belief, and so on and on. Because everybody is frightened.

But I think that this could also be a time of tremendous excitement and challenge. There's a wonderful bit of Christopher Fry, from a play of his called *Sleep of Prisoners*, that seems to encapsulate this possibility. It seems to me to be a clarion call to all of us living now:

The human heart can go to the lengths of God,
dark and cold we may be,
but this is no winter now.
The frozen misery of centuries
breaks, cracks, begins to move;
the thunder is the thunder of the floes,
the thaw, the flood, the upstart spring.
Thank God our time is now
when wrong comes up to face us everywhere,
never to leave us
'til we take the longest stride of soul
men ever took . . .
Affairs are now soul size.
The enterprise is exploration into God.
Where are you making for?
It takes so many thousand years to wake,
but will you wake
for pity's sake?

### Eternal Father, Strong to Save

Eternal Father, strong to save,
Whose arm doth bind the restless wave,
Who bidd'st the mighty ocean deep
Its own appointed limits keep:
*O hear us when we cry to Thee*
*For those in peril on the sea.*

O Saviour, whose almighty word
The winds and waves submissive heard,
Who walkedst on the foaming deep,
And calm amid its rage didst sleep:
*O hear us when we cry to Thee*
*For those in peril on the sea.*

O Holy Spirit, who didst brood
Upon the chaos dark and rude,
And bid its angry tumult cease,
And give for wild confusion peace:
*O hear us when we cry to Thee*
*For those in peril on the sea.*

O Trinity of love and power,
Our brethren shield in danger's hour:
From rock and tempest, fire and foe,
Protect them wheresoe'er they go:
*And ever let there rise to Thee*
*Glad hymns of praise from land and sea.*

*William Whiting (1825–78)*

# CICELY SAUNDERS

*There's really only one place to meet Dame Cicely Saunders: at St Christopher's, the hospice that was her dream. It is a huge building, busy but serene, housing not only scores of patients but helping hundreds more who are mainly cared for at home. It has a day centre, a chapel and a creche, and is lit up by her artist husband's vivid paintings.*

*She is now seventy-five – tall, formidable, still sparklingly vital and enviably sharp of mind – and she has spent most of her long life planning, raising funds for and having built what has become far more than an institution: St Christopher's has become the inspiration for a movement that has instilled a new respect all over the world for people who are dying.*

*'You matter because you are you, and you matter to the last moment of your life,' says Dame Cicely. And after an hour with her, you begin to realise that the most valuable moments of your life may well be those that come at the very end.*

Basically it wasn't a happy childhood, because there was a lot of tension at home. My mother didn't find life very easy. She tried, but she was a very closed-in sort of person who found it difficult to relate in an open, easy way, and therefore it was difficult to relate to her.

I got on better with my father. He was tough and very ambitious for us as children. I think he made me feel that if you want to do something, you just get on and do it. And he spent endless time trying to teach us – my two younger brothers and myself – cricket and tennis and all that sort of thing. He was an open kind of person, but also pretty unpredictable.

My beloved aunt and godmother was the really important, stable person of my life. She gave me all the right
books, in a home where we didn't go to church or anything
like that. Books about English saints, *The Secret Garden*
– which I still read – *Lamb's Tales from Shakespeare* . . .
all those things you need to be introduced to when you
are young. And lovely illustrations! I had a beautifully
illustrated *Water Babies*, for example. She just had a gift
for finding the right books.

I was sent off to boarding school when I was ten. My
godmother was the matron there, and that was really the
reason I got sent away so early. I remember when I was
punished, and got sent to bed for the day with nothing to
do, she quietly came up and dropped me in a book or two.
She was always there, very, very tactfully and quietly in the
background, always the same. She fulfilled for me some of
the roles that my mother didn't. Right to the end of her
life, she was an abiding presence.

But I wasn't happy at school, either. I was lonely and I
didn't know how to step out of my loneliness. I think there
are a lot of people like that. Only later in life, perhaps, you
come to realise that if you forget about yourself a little bit,
and are more concerned with the other person, then things
begin to work. I especially hated being sent to Roedean
from the age of fourteen. I was sent there by my father,
and he didn't even ask me if I wanted to go there! I was
cross about that.

When I was sixteen, I announced that I was an atheist.
I had been very uninspired by school chapel, although I
enjoyed singing in the choir; I was also reading Bernard
Shaw – and I wanted to revolt! But when I began to train
as a nurse, at the beginning of the war, I started to become
interested in religion again.

I bought a little paperback called *Good God* by somebody under the pseudonym of John Hadham, and that
book made sense to me. From then I was searching and
searching. I read Archbishop Temple; I listened to C S
Lewis when he was broadcasting; I listened to *The Man
Born to be King* by Dorothy Sayers – I was enormously

impressed by that. With my head, I was encompassing what I needed; yet it wasn't real for myself.

I hadn't always wanted to be a nurse. But I was always concerned about people, and having been unpopular myself at school, I had a feeling for people who felt rejected. I had one term of wartime Oxford – and it just seemed to be the wrong place to be. A friend went off to do nursing, and I thought, 'Goodness, that's the answer.' And so I waited to get into St Thomas's to do my training, and the moment I started, the moment I arrived, for the first time in my life I felt, 'I am in the right place, doing the right thing, at last.'

*To her dismay, Cicely suffered from severe back pain – and was forced to give up nursing. But she felt she knew now that caring for patients was the right place for her, so she decided to train as a medical social worker. She went back to St Anne's, at Oxford, to qualify for this new career.*

My parents' marriage was ending and it was an exhausting time for me. I had to give such a lot of support to my mother – find somewhere for her to live and cope with her bitter disappointment and sorrow. I often was impatient with her, I'm afraid. She did try; she did her best. She'd had a very tough upbringing herself, and there were people to whom she was enormously helpful. And after my father died, she found peace.

I was delighted that she came down to St Christopher's to convalesce after a cerebral haemorrhage in 1968. She was here for a week and everybody was able to spoil her. She said a lot of goodbyes – and then she had a sudden second haemorrhage and died, just like that. So she had a happy ending, and I was able to put her ashes together with my father's. I put 'In Him is our peace' on their grave, and then felt I could rest about them.

After my parents separated, and after I'd been invalided from nursing and done a very hectic year at Oxford, I was pretty tired out. I went on holiday with some evangelical

friends, who set out the very simple, basic facts that an
evangelical group will give an enquirer – and what they
said made sense.

We sang:

> Just as I am, though tossed about
> With many a conflict, many a doubt,
> Fightings within, and fears without,
> O Lamb of God, I come!

And I felt, 'Well, I can really say that; I *am* in a muddle
– but I want! And if all I have to say is "I want" and "I
am coming", this is it.'

I remember going off by myself and saying, 'Please
could it be *real* this time, and not just, somehow, me.'
And then I felt as if someone had said, 'It's all right: I
have done it.' It was a feeling as if I'd been turned round;
that I'd been battling into the wind all my life, the wind
had been battering my face – but suddenly the wind was
behind me.

It was a transcendental experience, I suppose. And
it's been like that ever since – although I've gone on
searching. I think that if you don't go on searching for
meaning, in the field that I am in, then you can't work
in it – because there are always things to challenge you:
Why should such-and-such happen? How can you really
have a God of love, and these things happen in this world
– this mother leaving her young children? And so on.

My own response, when I am asked how God can allow
all this suffering, is: He also suffered, and within His
suffering is the total commitment to us in our suffering.
And I think He comes into our lives in whatever way we
need, if we'll only ask and wait. And I think if you do
that, you somehow know it's all right, and that the end
will finally explain.

The text I would turn to is, firstly, 'In all their afflictions
He was afflicted,' and secondly, 'You will ask no questions,'
because the answers are going to be there, it's going to be
all right. I think we have to live with questions now; but
God lives the questions with you.

If there are enough of you, in an institution like a hospice, who are searching for meaning, then you can perhaps create a climate in which patients and families themselves can reach out to their own meaning. It's terribly important that we don't impose our meaning, that they must sing their own song, but we can perhaps give them space and an atmosphere in which they feel it's worth doing. And there are questions! Over and over again, you hear people say, 'It makes you think.'

After I suddenly realised that I believed with my heart as well as my head, I said, 'What do I have to do, to say thank You and to serve?' I didn't know for three years, so I just went on doing what I was doing, which was being a social worker. But then I discovered what I had to do to serve, through a Polish Jew I met in the first ward I took over when I got a job at St Thomas's.

*David Tasma was forty, and came from the Warsaw ghetto.*

He had no relatives and very few friends in this country. When he was discharged, I followed him up in out-patients, because I knew he had inoperable cancer. When he collapsed, his GP got on to me and said, 'I am admitting him to the local hospital.' I went to see him while he was waiting for the ambulance. I was actually the person who told him that he was going to die; I paid many, many visits in the two months between then and when he died.

David was an agnostic Jew who had very much lost his way – although his grandfather had been a rabbi, and had had him talking and talking about spiritual matters when he was a little boy.

One day he said to me, 'Can't you say something to comfort me?'

And because he was Jewish, I said the Twenty-third Psalm to him, *The Lord's My Shepherd.*

He said, 'Go on.'

So, as I was always singing in choirs, I said the *Venite.*

And again he said, 'Go on.'

I managed to dredge up another psalm, and then I said, 'Well, shall I read to you?'

And he said, 'No, I only want what is in your mind and in your heart.'

That was, of course, a very personal exchange – but thinking about it afterwards, this became one of the foundations of hospice: everything of the mind, together with the friendship of the heart.

While we were talking together, the idea of setting up a special home for people in his situation came into our talking. And when he talked about leaving me something in his will, he said, 'I'll be a window in your home.' He left me what came to £500 in his will, from an insurance policy. That's why the front of St Christopher's has this big window, with a plaque for him; it was the first gift to the hospice, given by David when he died on the 25th of February, 1948.

David's choice of a window commissioned us to openness. So that's another hospice foundation: openness to each other, as well as to the patients' families, and to the world.

Before he died, he said to his ward sister who passed it on to me, 'I've made peace with God,' with the faith of his fathers, although he didn't ask for a rabbi or anything like that. After he died, I was at a prayer meeting and I started to sing, *How Sweet the Name of Jesus Sounds* and I thought to myself, 'But it didn't to him.' And again I was *told*: that 'He knows Me far better than you do already.' I've never worried about anybody again, because I knew that, in the freedom of the spirit, he had found his own way. And that's what we want for our patients. You can certainly be a good atheist in the middle of St Christopher's, either as staff or patient, and know you're not a second class citizen.

So David had given me my commission: to do something for people like him; to help them search – as he had searched – to find the meaning in his life at the end; and also to help them have everything of the mind: everything that could help with pain, and all the other problems of weakness and dependence.

I found the loss of David very difficult to begin with. The moment that really helped above all was when I was on holiday with my father up in Scotland. I got up very early and walked along the loch on a lovely June morning, and sat down beside a little river running down with brown peaty water. And then I felt that I'd slipped right out of time: everything went quiet, and I knew I was in the eternal Now, and David was there somewhere. It didn't have to be close; it was quite all right as it was. I don't know how long that lasted, but then I came back into time and I heard the blackbirds singing and the water flowing. But I still knew that he was all right.

Love has many faces. Our whole relationship took place in a busy surgical ward – but I felt at the time that, if I never had anything else, that would be enough. And he had, of course, given me the commission of what I had to do.

*At the age of thirty-three, Cicely began a third training, this time to become a doctor, focusing particularly on controlling pain in patients terminally ill with cancer.*

I read medicine in order to do something about the control of pain in terminal illness. And I chose it because I saw something of a need that patients had for better treatment, but even more about the achievements they could make at the end of their lives if they had help.

At the time when I began planning St Christopher's, there were reports which showed that dying at home was full of pain, full of neglect. They revealed the really devastating, chronic illness of people having an awful time at home. But being in hospital was no answer. There was another report from the wards of a London teaching hospital showing a lot of unrelieved suffering. There were few places for people who were terminally ill. Either you stayed in a busy ward and you just got moved down to the end, or you were put into a single

room where doctors hated coming in, because they felt
they had failed.

Or you were sent to one of the earlier hospices, which
might well have beds awfully close together, might not
have the amount of privacy that you yearned to have,
and certainly didn't have care for the family, or long
visiting hours. District nurses were struggling on, nurses
in chronic hospital wards were struggling on, and they did
valiantly. But nobody had really got down to researching
how to get better and better at controlling distress at the
end of life; or researching how families feel, and what
the best way was to help them; how patients feel; or how
you could really listen, in a constructive and helpful way.
And nobody had really looked at whether you could take
hospice expertise to a patient where they really want to
be: in their own homes. There was very little in the way
of teaching.

Looking after terminally ill patients did seem to be an
untilled field. The surgeon I was working for said, 'Go and
read medicine; it's the doctors who desert the dying. And
there is so much more to be learned about pain, you'll
only be frustrated if you don't do it properly – and they
won't listen to you.'

Some of them did listen, and a great many of them have
done superb work themselves. But it can be awfully easy
to turn away when you feel you can't do anything. Patients
still come in saying, 'The doctor said there was nothing
more he could do.'

And that's a very sad thing to say, because there are
people who can do something. Palliative medicine is now
a recognised part of medicine as well as a recognised part
of human care. At St Christopher's we have never said
we were the first hospice, but we were the first to include
research, and teaching, and home care, and regarding the
family unit as the unit of care.

Sometimes families find it difficult to be involved, and
we need to be listening to them and their difficulties just
as much as we do the patient. We have a very strong social
work department, and our chaplain works with families a

great deal, and so do our nurses and doctors, of course. And we have far more patients at home than we have in St Christopher's, and there of course the family is the caring team.

When we had our twenty-fifth anniversary service in Westminster Abbey nearly two years ago, the Abbey was full, and nearly three quarters of the congregation were families of people who'd been in St Christopher's.

Because of all this, I think we have become a catalyst for a whole lot of people around this country – and now around the world – who are taking the basic principles which we tried to demonstrate. People are doing it in their own way in different cultures, bringing their own expertise. It's wonderful when you meet at an international conference, and you have people from Australia, Korea, Japan, South Africa, and so on. We have so much in common. I think what happened was that hospice emerged at a time when it was desperately needed and there were people who were prepared to do something about it.

A lot of people think that cancer is perhaps the worst thing to die of, because you can see death coming. Well, personally, I want to have time to say to people 'I'm sorry' and 'Thank you' and tidy things up a bit. So I think cancer can give you a horrible death but I think we know so much, much more that it need not be so horrible now. We can really control pain.

But there are pains that are really difficult: often there's a psychological problem, a family problem, all woven in together with the physical pain. I think you have to be learning all the time. Although we know much more now than we did before, we never, never want to say, 'We know everything.' We are ready to learn from other people and ready to share knowledge, always.

*The learning often came from the patients themselves.*

Towards the end of 1960, while I was still a medical

student, we had formed a charity and were beginning to get going on our plans for the hospice. I was talking about all this with a patient at St Thomas's, Mrs G., whom I knew for seven years as she died, very slowly, of a paralysis with blindness. She and I had been discussing the hospice all along the line, endlessly talking together, day by day. On this occasion, she said, 'What are you going to call it?'

I said, 'Well, I'm going to call it hospice, because I'm at St Joseph's Hospice now and that's a good word.'

And she said, 'What does it really mean?'

So I said, 'Well it's come to mean, mainly, a stopping place for travellers.'

'Oh, travellers,' she said. 'It will have to be St Christopher's, then, won't it?' And so it is.

Mrs G. was a very special person. Her name was Mrs Galton, but we remained 'Mrs G.' and 'Miss Saunders' throughout our whole seven years of friendship. I remember another patient coming out of Mrs G.'s room, saying, 'You can't even be sorry for her, she's so alive.' And there she was, blind and paralysed – she didn't even know which side she was on when you turned her – she couldn't have been more disabled: but she had her mind, and she had her intense interest in other people. And she, more than anybody, got me through my years of being a medical student and a house-man. She's certainly one of the founding patients of the hospice.

Her mother was always with her, except when she had a break to go on holiday. But we never had to arrange for other people to come in to visit instead, because they always just turned up. Mrs G. used to say, 'I wonder who's going to come this time?' And I remember her saying to me one day, 'You know, some people can read their Bibles and get their help there, and some people can go to church and get their help there, but He deals with me differently: He sends me people.'

It has been a long long friendship – or even, if you like, love affair – with patients all the time.

*Mrs G., Cicely's father, and Antoni, another Polish patient she fell in love with, all died between 1960 and 1961.*

I got my bereavements fairly well muddled up, I think, and I found it very difficult. I used to go down to a place in the country, over and over again, and partly work and partly birdwatch.

But watching others die can make the approach to one's own death easier. It has given me confidence that there is help; and I think the quiet running down of a death from a mortal illness is very different from the sometimes agonised, quick death of a heart attack. I've seen enough people with the feeling that they have gone somewhere – there's a moment when it is different. That 'somewhere' is a mystery, but it's somehow a safe mystery.

And so, although I may come up to my death with as much apprehension as anybody, and I expect I will, I will have some confidence in the people around, and I hope I will have the confidence to put my hand out to be grasped. Somehow you only have to try and put your hand out, you don't try and catch: I think God is the catcher.

Sometime after Antoni died, I'd been off in the car to get new records because I was still feeling sad. While I was in a line of traffic, I saw a picture of the crucifixion through the window of a gallery, and I thought, 'Goodness, I must go in.' I went in and I bought a small picture, *Christ Stilling the Storm*. I wrote to the artist, Marian Bohusz – another Pole! – to thank him for having painted such a picture, and I said I hoped, when we had built St Christopher's, that we would be able to have a larger one for our chapel.

And he wrote back and said this was the most important thing that had ever happened in his life, and invited me to come to his students' exhibition – and that's where we met. But we didn't get married for a very long time, because he was very much into his freedom, and painting, and all his pupils, and anyway his first wife was still alive in Poland. And I was very busy getting St Christopher's going. So we only married in 1980, but we are very together. And he is now ninety-three, but he sits back in his chair and says, 'I am completely happy.' And if you can do that when you are so disabled that you can hardly walk at all without being desperately breathless, it is quite something.

So there were three Polish men in my life, but all very different, who gave me different gifts. David gave me my commission, and a lot of help in getting going. Antoni and I met at a very deep level, very much at a spiritual level, and I was really devastated after he died because, of course, we didn't have any memories. It was such a very short time. And we hadn't done anything together except be in a six-bedded bay, sitting and talking and listening.

With Marian – I'm just with him all the time. I do look after him; I have quite a lot to do. But he's filled the hospice with lovely pictures, which are full of beauty – suns, forests, and also religious pictures. His paintings are also in the chapel here. There's a wonderful triptych: nativity, crucifixion and resurrection. I wanted the three together. I think it has given a tremendous amount of atmosphere to the hospice, and for him it has meant a place where his art is together – almost like the San Marco convent in Florence, if you can make that comparison. So we've been able to give each other a lot at the end of our lives.

And that can be a very good time in a marriage, when a lot of the fuss and fret is over. I think you have come to a place where you know yourself a bit better, and perhaps have come to terms with at least tolerating yourself. People can be absolutely maddening, and you have to be able to realise that you are too but that basically it doesn't matter. It's superficial, compared to the death of the relationship.

*Dame Cicely is a fierce opponent of legalising euthanasia.*

I think it would make a whole lot of vulnerable people,

consciously or unconsciously, think, 'I am nothing but a burden now, I ought to opt out.' Social pressures, possibly family pressures, are impossible to guard against. So I think the rule against taking life in that way should hold.

That's the negative reason. The positive reason is that we have seen how much people can achieve at the end of their lives. Some of them – after having said, 'I wish I could end it all!' in anger, and despair, and pain – have changed their minds. And they would have missed what they managed to find in those last times.

If someone is in such severe pain that they don't want to be alive any more, what you do is deal with the pain. And the pain is the pain of their mind as well as the pain of their body, and maybe the pain of their families. You do your best – and so far as our patients are concerned, people do not need to die in agony; they really do not!

Occasionally we may need to say, 'Would you like to be more sleepy, and just wake up for meals?' And sometimes people ask for that, and sometimes people say no. It's their choice. But the main thing is to say, 'I will not run away; I will come back and listen to you again; I will go on coming back; I will go on doing my best to help you come to terms with what you are going through.'

Although there are some people for whom one could feel euthanasia is the only solution, we are part of society: we cannot have something that's going to take freedom away from other people. It was Bernard Shaw who said 'Independence? That's middle class blasphemy. We are all dependent on one another, every soul of us on earth.' We are dependent, and I think the dependence is what holds us together as a society. And I think euthanasia would be a very great blow to that important cohesion.

A long time ago I was preaching at a boys' school. Over dinner afterwards, the headmaster reported on a discussion on euthanasia with the Upper Fifth, and he said they had come to the conclusion that 'euthanasia is emotionally attractive, socially dangerous, and should never be legalised'. I think it couldn't have been put better.

### Dame Cicely's mission

I've been lucky. I had a vision, which I felt I was given, and I was able to do something practical about it. It was a day by day business, but there was a vision – which I had to follow after in the most practical, definite, raising-money, learning, interesting-other-people way possible!

I think people need space to be themselves, people need to fight according to their lights, for how long they want to. It's not a question of whether you want them to 'go gently into that good night' or whether you want them to 'rage against the dying of the light': they choose. It's up to them. We need to remember the art of 'naive listening', of not having an answer when you first start listening to a person, but letting them do their own searching.

People do mind, as they come to realise they are nearing the end of their lives, how their relationships are: they look back on things which, perhaps, they wish they hadn't done. And although you can't change the past, I think you can sometimes change what it means. It's quite remarkable what people can do in a very short time. You see patients finding answers, you see families finding their own strengths. If you see people coming to – almost by definition – the most mature part of their lives, that's very rewarding.

It doesn't always happen, of course, and you get people who are angry and anguished right the way through. But it's surprising how often things come into place, and people feel that they can lay down their lives saying, 'Well, I'm me . . . and it's all right.'

There is an awareness that they are essentially themselves, when so much has been stripped away – and that they themselves, and their family, *matter*. And the closeness which we so often see is a gift. One feels that there is some kind of a grace there, which is difficult to put a hand on – but it's a meeting at a depth that they may never have achieved in the rest of their lives.

Dying people have, in a sense, a solidarity with all dying people everywhere, with all mankind. But so have we! And when we group around the people who are dying, we remember that we are just human too.

## Just As I Am

Just as I am, without one plea
But that Thy blood was shed for me,
And that Thou bidst me come to Thee,
O Lamb of God, I come!

Just as I am, though tossed about
With many a conflict, many a doubt,
Fightings within, and fears without,
O Lamb of God, I come!

Just as I am, poor, wretched, blind;
Sight, riches, healing of the mind,
Yea, all I need, in Thee to find,
O Lamb of God, I come!

Just as I am, Thou wilt receive,
Wilt welcome, pardon, cleanse, relieve:
Because Thy promise I believe,
O Lamb of God, I come!

Just as I am (Thy love unknown has
Broken every barrier down),
Now to be Thine, yea, Thine alone,
O Lamb of God, I come!

Just as I am, of that free love,
The breadth, length, depth, and height to prove,
Here for a season, then above,
O Lamb of God, I come!

*Charlotte Elliott (1789–1871)*

# EMMA NICHOLSON

*I talked to Conservative MP Emma Nicholson at her
large, comfortable home in a quiet Devon village. In
the week, she must commute to London and the House
of Commons but, whenever she can, she retreats to life
with her family.*

*But where should we talk? The conservatory is full
of light, but it is also the busy study of her husband, Sir
Michael Caine. The hall is wide, but houses Emma's
beloved piano: despite having to use a hearing aid,
she has never lost her passionate love of music. The
antique-filled drawing room is beautiful, but perhaps
a touch too grand. What about Emma's study? It brims
with papers – piles on her desk, more in boxes. Emma
is, after all, an irrepressibly active woman, with an
idealistic sense of service that gives her no respite.*

*So we crowd into the kitchen. Although it is large,
the space is filled by a vast family dining table, where
Emma dispenses generous helpings of old-fashioned
steak and kidney pie. But the table is moved and there
is space to talk . . .*

Music is fundamental to my life. I'm very behind on
my piano practice at the moment – and I've got an
organ recital soon, so I really must button down to a
bit of work.

I was lucky as a child because we always had a piano
in the house, and generally more than one: two, three –
even four, from time to time. I had a large number of
great-aunts who didn't get married until they were too
old to have children, so their possessions came to us when
they died. And that included pianos.

So from the first moment that I remember being alive,

there was a piano there for any of us to put a finger on and see what happened. Learning music came naturally because it was there from the start to be enjoyed and valued.

Sometimes it could be a little frustrating. I'm the third of four sisters, and my older sister could play wonderfully, much better than I could. And I've never forgotten my sister Harriet, who was much younger than the rest of us, striking the piano when she was just eighteen months or two years old – and bursting into tears. When she was asked what the matter was, she said, 'It doesn't do for me what it does for the others!'

I love singing: and the louder and higher, the better. I remember my poor mother – with four singing daughters – cowering with embarrassment in church. I think that the voice is the musical instrument that involves your body, your mind, your heart, your soul. With any other instrument, it is as if you're trying to harness and bring out a composer's thoughts – but your voice is yourself: it's your own, it's your innate musical instrument. I think all of us can communicate better with God when we're singing. It's such a natural outpouring of worship, of love, of happiness, of despair, of desperation, of anger, of joy – the voice gives everything.

At first, as a small child, I made a big fuss about going to church, complaining that it was far too boring. Then my mother put me in the choir, when I was three and a half, and that was a huge success. Music was my reason for going to church, and by the age of eight I was playing the organ there. Even now, music is the magnet for me: the words and thinking in church are so clearly man-made – there are clumsy human fingerprints all over it – but music allows you to worship in a direct line.

At Sunday school, my father was a church warden, one of two. Next door to us lived the other church warden, who was also our local Member of Parliament, Anthony

Hurd MP – Douglas Hurd's father. Church was very much a part of our lives.

*When Emma was ten, she went to a Church of England Convent School, St Mary's, Wantage.*

Up till then, I'd had a seamless religious education. On Sundays, nursery school turned into Sunday school, so school and religion were all-of-a-piece. But at St Mary's with the nuns, I began to have proper religious studies: I learned some Hebrew, Aramaic, Latin and Greek, which made the Bible much more interesting. And I learned comparative religion. There are many paths to God: it is a matter of luck which one we are born into; to exclude other people's religion is anathema to me.

The pattern of the day at St Mary's was set by the nine offices which the nuns plainsang in chapel, and I became the organist and head of the choir. So during my schooldays I had on offer a variety of forms of worship. In Wantage we had the chapel: spiky, incense, wonderfully high church. But in the church in town – which I often went to because the organist Mr Avery was totally blind, and I was one of the lucky ones who was allowed to help him get his music out and sit beside him on the organ stool – there was a wider variety of worship, including some that was not so high church. So there was a good mixture of Anglican, middle of the road worship. And at home in our tiny little village church of Winterbourne, we had whatever the current vicar had on offer. Maybe the best of these was the one who retired from being Chief of Police in Singapore, became a Christian, and then became our vicar. He was a wonderful vicar, except that when he dropped the Prayer Book, he couldn't remember the Lord's Prayer!

I'm sure that all of us are guilty of taking bits and pieces of religion to suit ourselves. Maybe the challenge is always to try to be cleaning the room that is your mind: trying to look at it all afresh and anew – even though I can't say that I manage it. But whatever style of worship we adopt, I think we have to be careful that it leads to the single purpose of worship, which is praising God.

*Emma, to no one's surprise, became a student at the Royal Academy of Music. But to everyone's surprise, she didn't do as well as she had expected, despite working diligently. After four years, very sadly, she had to leave, when the problem was finally uncovered . . .*

My mother had had German measles before I was born, and that had swiped a bit off the top of my hearing.

The word 'deaf' is an odd word. You don't say, if somebody is wearing glasses, that they are blind. But if you have the tiniest fraction of a loss of hearing, people promptly label you as deaf – and deaf in their terms means 'thick, out of touch, not a member of the human race, somewhere out in a far-off planet to be ignored'. Well, I'm not like that, and I'm not going to be seen like that either. Nor do I think that *anyone* who wears a hearing aid or has any form of hearing loss should be looked at like that.

But even to imagine that people who are profoundly deaf – which is the correct term for real deafness – can't enjoy music is a fallacy. God gave us several different ways of hearing: for example, there's bone hearing as well as the auditory nerve hearing. There are drummers who are totally deaf and yet can pick up the beat of the drum through their bones. So music can be an enjoyment and a happiness irrespective of our hearing, and it is even possible to be a creator of music: a performer or a composer. Think of Beethoven, who went on composing long after his auditory nerves had totally collapsed.

When I was at the Royal Academy, it was very

frustrating not to have access to modern hearing aids. Nowadays we have these tiny bits of pink plastic that I shove in my ear in the House of Commons – and take out again, sometimes, if I don't like what I hear! But these aids just didn't exist then, and that was frustration indeed. I couldn't hear the flutes properly, I couldn't hear the violins properly, and therefore I couldn't get the balance of the music right. Maybe that's why I play the organ a great deal. You pull out all the stops and the church rocks, whatever you do!

*Despite the shock and loss at having to leave the Royal Academy, with typical fortitude, Emma embarked on a new career: in computing. This was at a time when women were rarely seen in this field – especially women who had stopped doing maths at the age of eight! But Emma learned fast, and quickly became a senior software analyst. In Africa she helped a newly de-colonised government to organise its central computer system. And then she nursed her mother through cancer.*

I looked after my mother, with my three sisters, right to the end at home: it was a very important time for me. Maybe in the modern world we're too frightened of death. Perhaps because we have stopped worshipping God in such a formalised way, we have allowed ourselves to see death as something to be really scared of. In fact, death is a part of life, just as birth is a part of life. You have to go through the whole cycle. But it's a great deal easier to tolerate your own death than the loss of other people.

Losing others to death is a terrible thing. It's something I resent bitterly every time it happens. Every time, I'm very angry with God. A friend has just died who had been the chairman of the biggest children's charity in Poland, a wonderful paediatrician. Why did he get lung cancer? Why should he have to die? I'm angry and frustrated that other people go. I need them here: it's a very selfish reason. The Polish children will miss him terribly; perhaps I'm most angry for them.

I've never doubted God's existence but I have had enormous difficulty in coming to terms with evil in God's world: suffering, pain, grief, misery, aloneness. These seem to be inflicted on most of the human race.

When I was about twenty-one, I was taken by my father to visit a leper colony. It was in the middle of Africa and I've never forgotten it. My father jumped out of the Land-Rover and went straight forward, with his arms outstretched, to the lepers and started shaking their stumps. I went to follow suit – and saw the face of the first man he'd touched. He was just standing there, tears streaming down. And he said, 'Nobody ever touches us, nobody ever touches us.'

Leprosy was then thought to be infectious. I remember so well looking at these 750 men – they were all men – and thinking, 'These people have been totally rejected by society.' Watching them alone and friendless, knowing how much they all wanted to be back in their villages, in among the great life and laughter of an everyday African life . . . it was a sad and bitter experience.

Our own house here in Devon has a leper hole, left over from the twelfth century, when there was a leper colony in the next village. It's down in the basement; a tiny little room, very cold. When I look at the little shaft through which the leper's food came . . . ! Think of somebody living down there, maybe for twenty years or more, fed and watered but isolated, totally. That leper was outside human society.

And political ostracisation is just as horrible. I think we have to be very careful, in modern society, not to make lepers of different sorts of people; not to isolate communities with different styles who, for some reason or other, at a given moment in time, we don't happen to feel blend in with ourselves. We need to challenge our thinking – and reach out and embrace them all.

*After the death of her mother, Emma went to Poona, India, and was deeply impressed with the work of the Wantage nuns among the poor. When she came back to England, she went to the Save The Children Fund, hoping they would send her back to India, but they wanted her to help with their computer system. She initiated their polio immunisation programme (now run internationally by the World Health Organization) and, as Director of Fund-raising from 1977 to 1985, she raised their annual income from £3.5 million to £42 million. It was time to move on to yet another challenge: running for Parliament.*

There's no fun in doing anything easy. What's the point? The bigger the problem, the better: if it's too small, I can't motivate myself. The fun and excitement of life comes in identifying a mountain that is too high for you to climb – and beginning at the bottom. Once you've climbed that, look for the next one. I don't think that's some kind of personal punishment: that's fun, that's the game!

And failure is an essential part of achievement. If you can't build in failure, then you're not testing yourself enough: your goals aren't nearly high enough. Failure doesn't have to be failure in the sense that people think of it. Failure can be a part of the learning process: achievement is just the part that happened to go right. So having gone through twenty failures, and having learned a bit each time, on the twenty-first time you find it comes together – and then you must identify another challenge for yourself. People don't fulfil their potential because of their fear of failure – it's the gravest weakness of humans. My biggest bugbear is laziness, moral laziness.

And another thing about how one perceives failure. I think it's important to disentangle 'not doing what is expected of you' from 'not doing the best that you could have done at any single moment'. It may be that other people have unrealistic expectations of you, or the wrong expectations. Or perhaps they are seeking to force you to do something that they won't do themselves because they're cowards, or because it's not the right thing to do anyway.

I think the correct sense of failure, in the old fashioned sense of the word, is failing to do our best by our *own* perception of what the right thing to do is. But what does the word 'right' mean anyway? Maybe the greatest difficulty in life is in disentangling the right course of action.

And of course there are many occasions when I look back and think, 'If I'd worked just that little bit harder, if I'd been a bit more imaginative, if I'd understood that person better, I could have done something for them that would have made a difference!' And that's the pain that stays with me.

Maybe one of my first surgeries in this constituency hurt most of all. A lovely girl came to see me. She was a nurse, and she was also looking after a husband who was a quadraplegic, as well as two small children – and her life was impossible. We got on very well, and I thought of some things that would help her, and I promised her that we'd meet again in a week or two. She left. When I came back home, I said to Michael, my husband, that I would go and have tea with that girl. But I didn't. I was tired, I didn't want to go out again that evening, and it was a couple of hours' drive away. That night, she killed herself.

I think that, if I had gone, maybe just that little bit of thinking of something different, the excitement of talking about something else, might just have stopped her. I blame myself bitterly for that.

All of us should expect a great deal more of ourselves than we do. I don't think I've done more than a quarter of the things I could have done, helped more than a quarter of the people I could have helped, or achieved more than a very small fraction of the things that, maybe, were within my power or ability to achieve. I must try harder.

The great saints, the great figures who made Christianity – who identified it, who articulated it, who suffered for Christianity, who, in the pagan world of Rome and Greece, nonetheless were able to raise the flag and carry it forward – they really suffered: we're too comfortable.

*Emma became MP for Devon West and Torridge in 1987.*

Politics was very much a man's world: when I was elected, I held a celebration party in the Tavistock Conservative Club – which until that day had not admitted women.

In my twenties, when my father retired from Parliament, I said, 'That's it, now I can afford to think for myself!' Because I'd spent my childhood knocking on doors, saying, 'Vote for Papa' or 'Vote for Uncle Reggie' or 'Vote for Uncle David' – or for another half a dozen cousins. And I said to myself, 'That's it! Those are their views: now I'm going to think for myself.'

But it isn't always easy. In a sense, I think this kind of political courage is more demanding than the physical courage you need if you are being shot at or bombed. Political courage is different – and very, very tough, because what it means is ostracisation. You're out in the cold. Remember the old phrase 'beyond the pale'? It means you're pushed out of society, like a leper.

Maybe political courage is so difficult to practise consistently because politics is the framework and the fabric of so much to do with everyday life nowadays. The modern state is a very, very powerful animal – and each successive World War has empowered the winning states further, whether they are Conservative, Socialist, Communist or even Fascist. Therefore political chill is a real iceberg.

It is also difficult to handle because it means you, personally, are not accepted, and that's hurtful. Certainly I have felt the chill winds of my party, when I voted against

Mrs Thatcher for example. It made me feel very alone and very isolated.

And political courage rests upon your own personal judgement; it is really tough to sustain that against a barrage of colleagues who come at you – in a friendly way, in a not-so friendly way, in a very angry way, in a loving way – all trying to persuade you out of holding on to your own view. You have to hold very, very fast indeed against those excellent, rigorous thinkers – especially as all this questioning makes you keep saying to yourself, 'Well, am I really right?'

What upsets me most is thinking that I have made a wrong judgement and then hung on to it through obstinacy rather than through rigorous application of my intelligence; that upsets me most. It's not other people's opinions of me that count: it's my own opinion of myself.

I find politics is the most self-questioning trade of all. All the time, you're questioning yourself, you're questioning others. Maybe that's why it's so exciting: it is the cockpit of questioning. Very rigorous, great fun, and very, very challenging. And maybe that's also why such a high proportion of politicians worship God (it *is* a high proportion compared to the rest of the population): because we're right on the sharp edge of permanent self-analysis.

Politics is a difficult, difficult friend to have. What are your motives for being involved in politics: is it to serve – or to rule? Is it to be helpful to others – or to help yourself? And what about the corruption of power? 'Power corrupts; absolute power corrupts absolutely': it's very probably true. So politics is a very, very dangerous and difficult friend to acquire. But perhaps I'm lucky – backbenchers have no power at all!

I have always felt that religion and politics are two such potent things that they should not be mixed too closely together: they explode! Religion, the worship of God, should be a part of all of our lives. And the more that people who worship God take part in politics the better, as far as I am concerned. But I think you need to be really

careful not to allow political judgements to overwhelm
your religious views or vice versa: you must keep these
things separate. One is your professional life; the other is
the basis of your life, the entirety of your life. It is rather
as if you were going to say to a carpenter, 'Hey, be careful,
think about God when you're knocking that nail in.' He's
likely to go and hit his finger instead.

I don't call myself a religious Member of Parliament.
I'm somebody who worships God. I hope that we all
worship God. I would like everybody to know God and
to worship God because it brings such joy and happiness,
and because we are, after all, made in God's image. And
out of that, what I have to do is to use my best endeavours,
at all times, to carry out whatever job I'm doing to the
best of my ability. High standards; highest quality; best
efforts: that should be the thrust of all our lives at all
times, because that's the way to best reflect the image of
God. But it doesn't mean that I have a right to dump on
God the responsibility for myself voting the wrong way.
That's my job, not the job of the Almighty.

Why am I a Conservative when many of my views may
seem more Socialist? Although Socialism was undoubt-
edly founded on fine notions of brotherhood and hands
across the ocean, it somehow didn't come right in practice. I've never quite put my finger on why. It just
doesn't work.

Conservatism is full of flaws. It has no great central
philosophy that catches the mission spirit: it's really a
mixture of individuals' thoughts and beliefs – and therefore of human failings writ large. But for all its faults
and failings, perhaps because it comes from the genuine
grassroots, it can be made to work most effectively for
the people I care about.

And the people I care about are the ordinary people,
the people who haven't got a hotline to the powerful and
the important: the people who can't pick up the telephone
and get through to Number 10, Downing Street; the people
who are inarticulate – who may not have had a good
education and can't necessarily express themselves very

well, and who therefore can suffer beyond endurance with
no one knowing.

For some other indefinable, curious reason, I know
that Conservatism properly applied can do best for those
people. Improperly applied, of course it can be just as bad
as any other political belief.

*Emma found Amar in Iran, when he tumbled out of
a refugee truck – a small child burned by bombing
till he was barely alive. She tried to have him
medically treated in Iran but he had been too badly
injured, and so she brought him home.*

Our family has a slightly different shape now than the one
that Michael and I anticipated when we got married five
years ago. We hadn't thought that we would have a child
– and we now have Amar, who was injured in the uprising
following the Gulf War in Iraq.

Amar is twelve and is a Muslim, and that has brought
a whole different dimension into our world. It's a glorious
dimension. We love him enormously and he is a part of our
family – the central part of our family, come to think of it.

I have been working with members of the Muslim faith
for the last three years. It's been a whole new world for
me. I have been enchanted and delighted to discover how
closely Christianity and Muslim faiths intermingle. In fact the
three One God religions – Judaism, Islam and Christianity
– really are three brothers in the same family. Maybe that's
why we've fought so much over the many centuries!

But I think the time has come when we should get
above all those religious differences and come together,
because the three religions are so close, it's unbelievable.
They have the Muslim fasting period almost at the same
time as we have Lent; the only difference is those of the
Muslim faith seem to take it more seriously! Then the
celebration comes, in the same way as we have Easter.
And then there's another celebration around the time of
Christmas. There is also the pilgrimage in June, just about
the same time as we have Whitsun.

And I dare say that if I looked closely at Judaism, which I have never done, other than studying the Old Testament as the core of the emergence of Christianity, I'd probably find much the same there too. It's time we got together, instead of hating each other in this wretchedly old fashioned and outdated way.

I believe that when you learn about other people's faiths, you discover their ways to God. And they are to be honoured. Maybe the most damning indictment of Christianity has been our determination to encapsulate the path to God as only through our own faith. Tolerance is something that, perhaps, we have to teach ourselves all the time – every day, every moment of every day. Religious tolerance is the most fundamental tolerance of all for us to acquire and to teach other people, because faith and worshipping of God is central to every human being.

*Emma went out to Iraq in secret several times after the Gulf crisis.*

As a Member of Parliament, I found voting for conflict in the Gulf War a very harsh thing to have to do. So naturally I started to work for the victims.

I'd targeted my efforts in the deep south of Iraq simply because that's not a place where anyone else was working. I think it's of vital importance that you don't crawl all over everyone else's work and get in the way. I think that's an easy thing to do, to turn up where there is a problem that everyone is interested in and go away when the cameras don't happen to be there! The difficult thing is to work in places that are out of sight, out of other people's minds, and try to get something done.

That's why I've been concentrating very hard indeed on the marshes of southern Iraq. It is a form of hell on earth there just now. About half a million people were trapped in the marshes, who had been there since the uprising that followed the Gulf War. In other words, they rebelled against the atrocities of Saddam Hussain and, rather like the Jews who tried to rebel against Hitler, they have been wiped out as a result. It has been done invisibly, out of the Western media's sight, with no aid getting to them at all, other than the aid that the medical and food aid teams I've assembled have been taking in, and that of local religious groups.

It is very, very tough work indeed. We've already lost one man delivering aid inside the marshes, and I dare say we'll lose more. The bravery of the people carrying out this work is unbelievable. But the people inside are in such a desperate plight that we have to do everything we possibly can.

These dignified, articulate and highly intelligent people – the women, the children, the men – are under such a terrible strain of assault from Saddam Hussain. Looking at their battered bodies, that have been tortured . . . it's a very different world from here, where, if we touch each other, it is to help and heal. Someone touching a body *in order to hurt* is alien to most of our thoughts. It's a very tough thing to have to absorb and take into one's thinking.

### What does God mean to Emma?

I don't see God as an alternative to human relationships. I sometimes worry that in so much modern Christianity, God is taken up in place of people – people are asked almost to take God, or Jesus Christ, as a person who subsumes other relationships instead of using the love of God to serve and relate to others.

I personally believe that the relationships we have with other people – whether they're husbands, brothers, friends, sisters, cousins, uncles, children – are just reflections of the all-embracing relationship with God; and the better those relationships are, then surely the better our relationship with God. The failures we have with our human relations reflect a greater failure of a relationship with God.

I have no image of God because there should be no image of God. Yahweh, the word used to define God in the Old Testament, merely means 'the Unknowable'. We must not define God – therefore God should have no image. God is beyond that. God is everything. God is not an image, God is not a picture. The efforts we make to define God in painting, in music, in literature, in singing – they are just attempts to catch a fraction, a fragment, of the glory that shines out of God. For God is the earth, the world, the universe.

*The Day Thou Gavest, Lord, is Ended* brings one to evensong on a Sunday. What more can we do at the end of the day but say 'Thank you'? I love it. It's a wonderful hymn to play. You can really let rip on the organ and make the organ sing true. I usually play it in A flat major, a glorious key. It can be as rich as you like it, and yet it's easy for people to sing and that's a great help. It's really community worship.

And the words are so lovely too. It goes on to say that, as we go to sleep, others in another part of the world are waking up and are starting to praise God. I think, then, of my friends in the marshes who worship God through Islam, of my friends here who are Christians, of those in other parts of the world who are in trouble or joy, who are all one. The hymn brings the world together in worshipping God, and that's how it ought to be.

## The Day Thou Gavest, Lord, is Ended

The day Thou gavest Lord, is ended,
The darkness falls at Thy behest;
To Thee our morning hymns ascended,
Thy praise shall sanctify our rest.

We thank Thee that Thy Church unsleeping,
While earth rolls onward into light,
Through all the world her watch is keeping,
And rests not now by day or night.

As o'er each continent and island
The dawn leads on another day,
The voice of prayer is never silent,
Nor dies the strain of praise away.

The sun that bids us rest is waking
Our brethren 'neath the western sky,
And hour by hour fresh lips are making
Thy wondrous doings heard on high.

So be it, Lord; Thy throne shall never,
Like earth's proud empires, pass away;
Thy kingdom stands, and grows for ever,
Till all Thy creatures own thy sway.

*J. Ellerton (1826–93)*